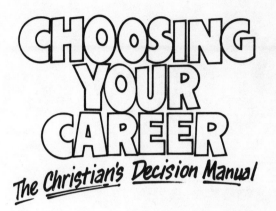

CHOOSING YOUR CAREER

The Christian's Decision Manual

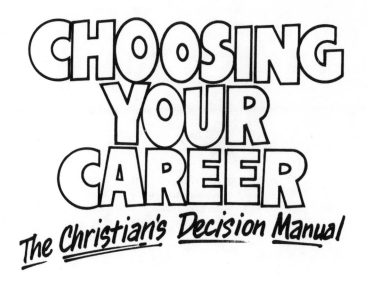

CHOOSING YOUR CAREER

The Christian's Decision Manual

MARTIN E. CLARK

BAKER BOOK HOUSE

Grand Rapids, Michigan 49506

ISBN: 0-8010-2483-8

Second printing, April 1983

Scripture citations are from the
New American Standard Bible
and the King James Version

Printed in the United States of America

For my wife,

Bonni

Contents

Preface

"I've never wanted to plan my life. All I've wanted to do since my salvation is to let the Lord lead me each day. Now look at the mess I'm in."

The young lady sitting in my office was about to be graduated from a major state university, and she had no idea what God's plan was for her profession. While her motive of following Christ daily was undoubtedly commendable, she had not recognized a number of things that God had done in her life, on a daily basis, that pointed toward His plan for her vocationally. She had shown plenty of evidence of a genuine commitment to Jesus Christ, but she had overlooked the necessity to make plans in a God-honoring manner.

This book was written to assist Christians who want to know what is involved in a career decision, and who want to make that decision in a way that pleases God and edifies themselves and others. The procedures outlined in its later chapters are not meant to replace the Lord's leadership; rather, they are a vehicle for recognizing His lordship and implementing His direction.

Too frequently, like the young lady already mentioned, Christians fail to set goals for themselves. They think that doing so would somehow make them insensitive to God's leading. Goal-setting, of course, *can* be an act of rebellion. But it is not necessarily so. The real issue is this: How does the Lord direct? By a feeling? a special set of circumstances? a religious hunch? Often, what some call the "Lord's leadership day-by-day" is no more than an excuse for living a directionless life. Instead of an evidence of piety, it is a clear symptom of poor stewardship.

The Bible gives numerous examples of direction and goal-setting in the lives of the faithful. From the Old Testament comes the example of Abraham, whose life at first appears to be a series of aimless wanderings. Was this hero of faith without a goal in life? Not at all. All his pilgrimages were explained in the summary, "he was looking for a city which had foundations, whose architect and builder is God" (Heb. 11:10). He had a goal, and his efforts revealed his attempts to reach that goal.

In the New Testament, the apostle Paul is a good example of one who set goals and made plans. His Epistles show his goals: "I press on toward the goal for the prize of the upward call of God in Christ Jesus'' (Phil. 3:14); ''I determined to know nothing among you except Jesus Christ and Him crucified'' (I Cor. 2:2); ''I am eager to preach the gospel to you also who are in Rome'' (Rom. 1:15).

But the supreme example of one who lived a goal-oriented life is the Lord Jesus Christ. He often stated His goal, once expressing it as seeking and saving the lost, once as granting abundant life. His entire incarnate experience was ordered to contribute to the accomplishment of His plan. When His disciples urged Him to assert Himself in a manner that would not contribute to His goal, He responded, ''My hour is not yet come.'' Then, on the eve of the crucifixion, He prayed to His Father, ''Father, the hour has come; glorify Thy Son, that the Son may glorify Thee'' (John 17:1). Jesus Christ had a definite goal; He did not merely drift aimlessly through His experiences, merely responding to His environment.

It should be clear, then, that a planned and orderly life pleases God, so long as the plan is God's plan. The emphases on self-discipline and exercise in godly practices found throughout Scripture assume that the believer has goals for which such exercise is appropriate.

The choices facing any young person demand thoughtful consideration and planning. Whether deciding about his education, career, life-style, or marriage, the serious Christian frequently asks, ''How can I find God's will for my life?'' Too often, the only answer given is, ''Just let the Lord lead you.'' This answer, though well meaning, is no answer at all; it is merely a restatement of the question. The sincere inquirer is not questioning whether the Lord should lead him. He has settled that issue already. What he needs is help in identifying the Lord's leading. This book advances practical suggestions, based on biblical principles, for the Christian who has committed himself to following God so he can recognize God's leadership.

Secular education leaders have articulated the need for career education, and an emphasis on careers has become the major movement in public education during this decade. This thrust is understandable, for when educators were faced with multitudes of graduates who had no skills qualifying them for jobs, a natural response was to attempt to meet the challenge. The career education movement in public education correctly acknowledges that the educational process must relate to all of life and must make a practical contribution to life. But this movement raises problems for the Christian. Secular education approaches life in a humanistic manner, and secular career development theories are totally human-centered. Career choices, as well as other life decisions, are approached with the assumption that man is the highest authority and that human satisfaction is the highest good. The

Christian, however, knows that God exalts only those who are subservient to Him. The Christian also knows that God has a plan for his life. But that fact would startle a secular career educator, for it violates every tenet of his humanistic philosophy.

Christian students who are being continually exposed to secular, humanistic career education need to see that their life goals must reflect their Christian faith. This book provides a re-orientation to goal-setting and career decisions from a biblical perspective. Its aim is to assist believers in making career decisions that glorify God in both process and outcome, thereby contributing to abundant Christian living.

I acknowledge with gratitude the contributions of Dr. Jay Adams and Mr. James Grier in reviewing portions of this manuscript and making valuable suggestions. Their insight has expanded and challenged my thinking on several of the topics presented in the following pages.

1 *Foundation Principles*

Living a God-planned life requires thought. The wild, emotional abandon that many equate with spiritual fervor does not produce faithful living. Rather, a commitment to God resulting from an understanding of His Word produces both the basis and the motivation for a God-honoring life.

Since this God-planned living requires thought, it is imperative that we examine our presuppositions about God and about ourselves. These considerations are foundational. Without them, the whole idea of God's will for our lives is absurd.

THINKING ABOUT GOD

God Is Personal

The God who really exists has disclosed Himself in Scripture as a personal Being. He is not merely a force, an idea, or a grand source of cosmic energy. Within the Godhead, the persons of the Trinity manifested their nature as personal Beings by both loving and communicating prior to their creation of the universe (cf. Gen. 1:26 and John 17:24). By using the plural pronouns to refer to God I am not denying the essential unity of the Godhead, but I am asserting the parallel truth within the trinitarian mystery—that somehow the distinct persons of Father, Son, and Holy Spirit exist within that unity. And both in unity and in diversity, the Creator of all that exists is personal.

Whatever else may be meant by man's creation "in the image of God," the "image" is most assuredly shown in the fact that we too are personal beings. Our personal nature is comprised of intellect, emotion, and will. This "image of God" in man allows communication between God and mankind, and indeed, Scripture records that this communication has occurred throughout man's existence. The very fact that God has revealed Himself in an inspired Scripture assures us that He is concerned about communication with us. We should therefore not fear that He would obscure His plan for our lives, or otherwise erect hindrances to our discovering His will.

This personal God actively involves Himself in His creation, especially in the lives of those He has redeemed. Although this is the clear teaching of Scripture and has always been believed by the true church, it is ridiculed by modern secularists as an antiquated, superstitious crutch. They view man as his own authority, wholly autonomous in making decisions, accountable to no one except himself and/or his peers (society, the state, etc.). The idea that God would "lead" or "call" someone is totally outside of the thought systems of those who have rejected the concept of a personal God. "If a god exists," the secularist thinking goes, "then 'it' is a cosmic force, a first principle, or a nebulous rationale for existence." Obviously, nothing like this could "lead" or "call" anyone to do anything.

But those who have accepted Scripture know that the true God is the personal Creator who still is active in His creation. Psalm 32:8 is more than empty rhetoric when it records God's promise, "I will instruct you and teach you in the way which you should go; I will counsel you with My eye upon you." The three verbs in this verse (instruct, teach, counsel) all point to a personal guiding activity by the Creator for the creature.

Numerous Scripture passages assure us of God's concern for every facet of our lives, from the momentous to the trivial. For instance, He numbers our hairs (Matt. 10:30) and records our tears (Ps. 56:8). He knows our sorrows (Exod. 3:7) as well as our movements, thoughts, and life patterns (Ps. 139:2-6). Since nothing in our lives escapes His notice and concern, we should expect Him to be personally involved in the overall direction of our lives. His concern over details makes no sense at all unless He uses those details to accomplish specific goals. And what joy this truth sparks in believers—the eternal God knows us personally and has a plan for our lives!

God Is Orderly

This basic assertion is so simple that it may seem simplistic; but it is undeniably true and extremely important. The God who really exists is neither confused, nor the author of confusion. He works according to His predetermined plan, without variation. His plan includes specific schedules, as illustrated by the fact that He sent His Son in "the fulness of time" (Gal. 4:4). He works all things according to His good pleasure, which is neither capricious nor changeable. If God were not orderly, His revelation regarding future events would become either meaningless or absurd; but since He is orderly, He can be seen to work all things toward this predetermined end.

We can understand God's orderliness best by contemplating His sovereignty. Our lives frequently lack order because either we encounter unexpected circumstances or we feel powerless to accomplish our objectives in a given situation. Further, we often misinterpret the past, do not understand our present, and certainly cannot discern the future. But these constraints pertain to us since we are creatures, and they are irrelevant to the sovereign Creator.

God's sovereignty clearly marks Him as Creator, distinguishing Him from all His creatures. The term "sovereignty" refers to God's perfection by which He does what He wishes to do. He encounters no surprises, nor is He ever frustrated by a lack of power to accomplish His will. He not only knows the past, present, and future—He *is* the Alpha and Omega. As sovereign, He does not leave His will to be accomplished by "accidents of nature," by random circumstances, or by whims of depraved men. On the contrary, He is the One "who works all things after the counsel of His will" (Eph. 1:11).

God's sovereignty, and the resulting order, is easily seen in His control of the stars and the other celestial bodies of the universe. Indeed, "the heavens are telling of the glory of God, and the firmament is declaring the work of His hands" (Ps. 19:1). God has ordained the pattern of these bodies so surely that astronomers can know what the sky looked like into which Abraham gazed. The psalmist was astonished by God's control when he wrote, "When I consider Thy heavens, the work of Thy fingers, the moon and the stars which Thou hast ordained, what is man that Thou dost take thought of him?" (Ps. 8:3-4). Among the many weighty truths in this passage is the one in the implied question, "Does God think about man, who seems comparatively insignificant, in the same manner He thinks about the stars when He ordains their courses?" The term "ordained" is the key to the answer. The inspired writer uses the same word in Psalm 37:23 to assure us that "the steps of a man are established [ordained] by the Lord, and He delights in his way." God's work in our lives is no more left to chance than is the pattern of the universe. In fact, the apostle Paul was writing on a very personal level about faithfulness in Christian living when he stated, "it is God who is at work in you, both to will and to work for His good pleasure" (Phil. 2:13). Because God exercises His sovereignty throughout His creation, we are not surprised when we read the promise, "God causes all things to work together for good to those who love God, to those who are called according to His purpose" (Rom. 8:28).

Since God is orderly, we who have been created in His image and then recreated by His grace should reflect order in our lives. Since God works according to plan, His new creatures might be expected to work according to plan also. The fact that we are not sovereign and therefore cannot perfectly imitate God's orderliness should not keep us from acting responsibly in following the Lord as faithfully as possible. When we realize that we bear the image of God, we will want to find and fulfill His plan for our lives in an orderly fashion. Living in a chaotic manner hardly testifies to the true nature of God. But planning, by itself, is not enough. Orderly living is pleasing to God only when the living conforms to God's order.

Living a God-planned life is thrilling, and it is possible because God is both personal and orderly. He has a meaningful plan for our lives, and He communicates with us so that we can know His plan.

THINKING ABOUT OURSELVES

Susan had grown up in a fine church, had gone forward in a church service invitation as a young girl, and had served her church as a youth group officer and choir member. Now a bright university student, she had come to my office because she was confused about fulfilling God's plan for her life. ''I pray,'' she related, ''but, Pastor, it seems as if God is very remote from me. I don't know what the problem is, but we're just not communicating, and the more I think about His will, the more confused I become.''

As we talked about her experience, it became increasingly clear to both of us that Susan had never really been saved. Instead of trusting Jesus Christ as Savior, she was trusting something she had done, her act of walking forward in a church service. The more she thought about it, the more she became convinced that her early ''salvation'' was no more than an emotional act which she went through only because her girlfriends were doing it. Unquestionably, God's will for Susan's life at that point was for her to be saved. Happily, she saw her need, repented of her sinful self-righteousness, and trusted in Jesus Christ for salvation.

Am I Saved?

The biblical promises about God's leadership are given to God's people, not to those rebelling against Him. This is not to say that God has no will or plan for unbelievers, for Scripture plainly teaches that an eternity of torment awaits those who persist in their unbelief. In addition, God uses wicked individuals to fulfill His plan in spite of their sin (Rom. 9:22-23), as illustrated by such persons as Pharaoh (Rom. 9:17) and Nebuchadnezzar (Jer. 25:9, 12). But God's use of these and other unbelievers certainly differs from His personal leadership of those who confess Him as Lord. S. Maxwell Coder has expressed this truth well:

> The cloud which directed the people of Israel in their way brought nothing but confusion to the Egyptians (Exod. 14:19, 20). Before anyone can expect to be led through the wilderness of this world by the

modern counterpart of the pillar of fire, he must be sure he is numbered among those to whom the promise is addressed. "What man is he that feareth the Lord? Him shall he teach in the way he shall choose" (Ps. 25:12).[1]

David's tumultuous life no doubt drove him many times to fall completely upon the guidance of God, and on one occasion, he prayed,

Let me hear Thy lovingkindness in the morning;
For I trust in Thee;
Teach me the way in which I should walk;
For to Thee I lift up my soul (Ps. 143:8).

David acknowledged in his prayer that trusting God was prerequisite to receiving guidance.

Any doubt about salvation needs to be removed before any progress can be made in knowing or doing God's will. Questions such as the following may be helpful in determining your salvation status:

Have I ever repented of my sin and claimed Christ's forgiveness?

Did I accept Christ, or did I merely go through a religious ritual because it was expected of me?

Do I now trust in Jesus Christ, or in something I have done?

Does my life show any spiritual development or evidence of salvation?

You are saved if you have repented of your sins and have claimed in faith Jesus Christ as your Savior. You must trust in His perfect righteousness for your standing before God, not in your own faulty self-righteousness. You must accept salvation as God's gift, and thereby renounce any thought of earning God's acceptance by your own effort.

It would be both futile and absurd to ask God for leadership while still rebelling against His will regarding salvation. The saved person, however, knows his relationship with God is correct, and he may confidently claim God's promises for guidance.

Am I Obedient to God's Word?

God has disclosed His will in Scripture. Although the Scripture does not explain everything about God's will (Deut. 29:29), it does tell us what God wants us to know and is the standard to which we are accountable. Consequently, when we ask to know more about God's will, we are assuming a responsibility to learn from and subject ourselves to His Word, the Bible. To do less would be presumptuous indeed, for we would be asking God to

---

1. S. Maxwell Coder, *God's Will for Your Life* (Chicago: Moody Press, 1949), p. 12.

reveal His will while at the same time we ignore what He has already revealed.

It is true that the Bible does not contain a specific answer to each specific question we may face, but we are mistaken if we use that truth as an excuse to neglect the Scripture. Consistent, systematic Bible study will develop our knowledge about God, about ourselves, and about basic principles which may be applicable to our question. If a specific verse does not answer our question, often a biblical principle gleaned from many passages will give appropriate guidance. Also, reading Scripture has an effect on our minds when it enlarges our understanding of God, and it is through such knowledge that God has granted all we need to live a godly life (II Pet. 1:2-4). Consequently, the psalmist exclaimed, "Thy Word is a lamp to my feet, and a light to my path" (Ps. 119:105).

Once again, attitudes toward God and His Word are of paramount importance, and these attitudes are revealed by our priorities. A typical example may highlight the attitude of distorted priorities. A student may be praying for God's guidance in a decision concerning his college major. At the same time, he may know from his Bible study that God's will for him as a new Christian is to be baptized and join a Bible-centered church, but he may be neglecting these imperatives or inventing excuses for avoiding them. So he has placed himself in quite a bind, his priorities showing a faulty attitude. While refusing to follow what God has already revealed through Scripture to be His will in one area of life, the student piously asks God to disclose His plan for another area of life. A faithful attitude, on the other hand, is one that orders priorities so that we are doing what we already know to be God's will before asking Him to reveal more.

Am I Delighting in the Lord?

> Delight yourself in the Lord;
> And He will give you the desires of your heart (Ps. 37:4).

How do we know if we are delighting in the Lord? Obviously, God does not give us every desire of our hearts (fortunately!), and so the condition upon which this promise is based is very important.

The word "delight" means "to find pleasure" or "to find happiness." We are therefore instructed to find our happiness in God Himself—in His Being, perfections, person. The essential point seems to be that we are not to seek greatest satisfaction primarily from created things, but rather, from the Creator Himself. Rather than making the desires of our hearts our primary focus in life, we are to concentrate on the Lord Himself, and He will then assume the responsibility of granting all we need for life and godliness. Jesus Christ spoke in the same vein when He challenged His disciples, "Seek first His kingdom, and His righteousness; and all these things shall be added to you" (Matt. 6:33). The "things" Christ referred to are listed earlier in the passage: food, drink, clothing—the primary objects of desire for the Gentiles (6:25, 31, 32). But when we personally identify with the Lord and seek to honor Him, He "adds" these things to our lives. The word "adds" is instructive, for it shows that one who focuses his life on the Lord has his identity determined thereby, and the "things" of this life do not determine identity but are merely added to an already fulfilling life.

When we "delight" in the Lord, we should expect God to grant the desires of our hearts. That expectation arises, not because we have placed God under obligation to us, but because our "delight" has so influenced our desires that they are in agreement with His will for us. The psalmist is here challenging us to order our priorities so that the eternal God Himself is of greatest importance to us, resulting in a reordering of lower "desires" to conform to that top priority. When this process begins to occur, we can pray with greater confidence regarding our "desire." Reordered spiritual priorities assure us that we are not asking amiss, merely to consume it on our lusts (James 4:3).

The application of the truths of Psalm 37:4 to the career decision is clear. Making the career decision itself our highest priority, the consuming passion of our lives, means that we are not delighting in the Lord and are exempting ourselves from the promise of this verse. When we make Him and our relationship to Him the highest priority, then we should expect Him to so work in our desires that they begin conforming to His will. To allow confusion over a career choice to interrupt Bible reading, prayer, or fellowship with the Lord is a grave mistake, for this rupture of relationship will surely distort our desires and lead only to frustration. Knowing God's will comes from knowing God well. As a husband and wife grow in their relationship until they often can accurately predict each other's desires without any new verbal communication, so we too can develop an anticipation of what God wants by seeking to understand Him better. Our desire for God's will can never replace our desire for God.

Frequently, students have told me, "I know what I want to be. But I do not want my will, I want God's will." This apparent difference between man's will and God's will arises from a basic mistrust of our own desires, and that mistrust is proper in its place. Jeremiah warned, "The heart is more deceitful

7

than all else and is desperately sick; who can understand it?'' (17:9). But Jeremiah was addressing people who were consciously rebelling against God, not those attempting to delight in Him or those in whom God's Spirit had begun mind-renewal (Rom. 12:1-2). Also, we recall Christ's prayer in Gethsemane, ''My Father, if it is possible, let this cup pass from Me; yet not as I will, but as Thou wilt'' (Matt. 6:39). At first glance, this seems to record a difference between the wills of the Father and the Son, with the Son surrendering His will to the Father. Upon reflection, however, we see that such an interpretation is unthinkable, since it suggests disagreement among the persons of the Godhead. Christ was probably affirming His unity with the Father's will, in spite of the great cost. Certainly, it is not the picture of the Son surrendering a rebellious will to His Father. Consequently, this passage does not establish the surrender of a rebellious will as the ideal, but rather, gives an example of consistent oneness of purpose with the Father.

Prior to salvation, our desires should be mistrusted, but in an unsaved state, we haven't the spiritual insight sufficient to question them. After salvation, we need to examine our desires to check their conformity to God's revealed will in Scripture; but at the same time, we need not assume that every personal desire violates God's will. We should expect that part of God's direction in our lives would be a transformation of our desires so that He acts in perfect accord with His will when He grants them.

Have I Committed Myself to Do God's Will?

When we learn to delight ourselves in the Lord, the next challenge found in Psalm 37 becomes easier to meet.

Commit your way to the Lord,
Trust also in Him, and He will do it (Ps. 37:5).

We ''commit'' our way to the Lord when we, literally translated, ''roll our way over onto'' Him. The psalmist described this commitment by using the synonym ''trust'' in the same verse. When we roll the burden of our ''way'' onto the shoulders of our Burden-bearer, we are confessing our own inability and trusting Him to take the leadership. We trust both His ability and His interest to accomplish what is best for our lives.

This commitment is to the Lord Himself, not to some specific plan for the future. The difference between the two may be illustrated by the student who says, ''But what if I don't like God's plan for my life?'' Such a statement reveals that this student will commit himself to a specific course of action, if he approves of it, but has not yet committed himself to the Lord. He has established himself as a censor of God's plans, to follow those he likes and to reject all the rest. God does not make His will known so we can negotiate with Him about it. He makes it known so that those who have committed themselves to Him will be able to obey confidently and eagerly. A commitment to God Himself presupposes the knowledge that God's will is perfectly good and completely wise. It is a commitment that acknowledges that God will not lead astray, that He will provide the necessary resources, and that He is entirely qualified to direct our lives.

Some speak of this commitment as "surrender," and that might be an appropriate designation if the individual has been consciously rebelling against God's known will. "Surrender," however, may not accurately describe the commitment of a person who is following Psalm 37:5, for a sincere inquirer is not ending a rebellion against God. He is, rather, seeking to know God's will so that he may align his own desires accordingly. Such is not a surrender, which implies defeat, but is an affirmation, which implies victory.

Isaiah provided the classic example of genuine commitment to the person of God in the inspired record of his own call as a prophet (Isa. 6:1-13). Following his vision of the infinitely exalted and holy God, Isaiah became aware of his own sinfulness. Aware that he could not approach God, let alone serve Him, in that state, he must have been encouraged when he received cleansing through the ministry of the altar, where innocent animals were offered as substitutes for the people's sins. Then he heard God's voice saying, "Whom shall I send, and who will go for us?" To this inquiry, Isaiah responded, "Here am I. Send me." He was yet unaware of the mission, but he was committed to the person of God to such an extent that he trusted God implicitly. In the same manner, we who have been graciously cleansed through Christ's atonement must trust Him in such a way that we say, "Wherever He leads, I want to go."

Trust in God Himself minimizes fear of the future, for it acknowledges that God is sovereign. Sometimes we fear because we are uncertain what God's plan will involve, and so we may fear failure. We fear because we know our frailties; we know only too well that we make mistakes. But the thirty-seventh psalm deals with this fear effectively:

> The steps of a [good] man are established by the Lord;
> And He delights in his way.
> When he falls, he shall not be hurled headlong;
> Because the Lord is the One who holds his hand (37:23-24).

We may err when trying to follow God's leading, but when that occurs, God deals with us as mistaken children rather than as hardened rebels. He assures that our fall will not be fatal. He holds our hands so that even the fall is within His control, and He uses our errors to challenge and strengthen us. This process may be likened to parents teaching children to walk. Knowing that a child will fall many times while learning to walk, the parent does not abandon the youngster or chastise him if he falls while trying. The parents will usually do all they can to make sure the inevitable stumbles do not hurt the child, often teaching the child on the softest rug available. Every effort is made to make each try both safe and profitable. S. Maxwell Coder likens learning to walk with the truth of Psalm 37:23-24 in this way:

> God is our heavenly Father. He watches our steps with great interest and tender compassion. When we fall, in our weakness, He gently restores us to our place, so that we are not utterly cast down. Stern measures may sometimes be required, if we repeatedly demand our own way; but if our delight is in Him (v. 4), then His delight is in us (v. 23). Thus, our weakness and God's strength are found linked together in what the Bible teaches about His program for our lives. Our tendency to fall is met with His desire to lead us by the hand.[2]

When we are conscientiously trying to do God's will, He will not allow us to go too far astray.

What Do I Understand?

Solomon's wisdom focused on God's guidance in the following proverb:

> Trust in the Lord with all your heart.
> And do not lean on your own understanding.
> In all your ways acknowledge Him,
> And He will make your paths straight (Prov. 3:5-6).

Having trusted in the Lord and committed ourselves to do His will, we yet need a knowledge of what His will is. Solomon warns against trusting our own understanding. His warning, however, cannot contradict other passages which challenge us to develop a spiritual understanding (Prov. 2:3; 4:7), and so he is not advocating abandoning reason to act on impulse or emotion. What concerned Solomon was the result of relying solely on human, unenlightened understanding. Consequently, early in his reign, he had asked God for special wisdom.

How do we know whose understanding we are leaning on? Fortunately, the two understandings do not have to be completely separate. Although we cannot completely think God's thoughts, He has revealed Himself in Scripture and that revelation can shape and develop our understanding. When we

---

2. Ibid., pp. 39-40.

immerse our minds in His Word, we can be assured that our understanding is no longer entirely our own. Instead, we should expect to be able to exercise an increasing amount of godly insight as His revelation renews our minds.

An enlightened understanding is demonstrated by acknowledging Him in all our ways. This acknowledgment is more than a theoretical affirmation that God rules. It is a faith at work, a living demonstration that God's Word has molded our minds to effect right behavior. To these faithful ones comes God's promise that He directs to the correct end, removing hindrances from the way.

Conclusion

Learning God's will and living it are neither simple nor easy. A checklist approach simply will not suffice, and neither this chapter nor the following ones are meant to deal with the topic in that manner. Rather, we must acknowledge that God-planned living grows out of a relationship between God and ourselves, and that this relationship must retain top priority. Knowing God, and learning to obey the will He has already revealed in Scripture will expand our understanding so that we can discern those things about His plan which He has not revealed as directly. Following God's leadership requires intelligent commitment to search daily for the evidences God places in our lives to show us His way. And in the entire process, our ultimate goal is to glorify God, realizing that His guidance is for our good only because it is first of all for His own glory.

QUESTIONS FOR PERSONAL INVENTORY

1. In order to trust our desires, we need to be delighting in the Lord (Ps. 37:4). List three behaviors that would demonstrate that you are delighting in Him.

   1.

   2.

   3.

2. Sometimes we hesitate to commit ourselves unreservedly to Christ for fear He will require us to do something we don't want to do. List the three careers that you most frequently fear God might require you to enter.

   1.

   2.

   3.

3. For each answer to question 2, list the specific factors of each career you dread the most.
   career 1:

   career 2:

   career 3:

Now, review the chapter and apply what you know about God to these dreaded activities. Can you count on God to change your desires and fears?

2 The Christian Value of Work and Career

Why should people work? At first, the answer may seem simplistically clear—to make a living. But is that the only reason? Why do people who have more money than they could possibly spend in five lifetimes continue to work, start new businesses, and continue producing? Some may merely be greedy, but often such persons demonstrate extreme generosity. Work must have some meaning in human life beyond acquisition of wealth. If work is an integral part of one's life, and it is, then the Christian should expect to find some guidance in the Word of God regarding the value of work in his life.

What Is Work?

"Work" generally may be defined as purposeful activity, physical or mental, in which one exerts himself. Such a definition corresponds both to the biblical concept of work and to the currrent use of the word. Also, one's "work" is often considered as a synonym of one's "career."

The "Puritan work ethic" has frequently been criticized as an antique hindrance to self-actualization in our present age. The technological advances of our society produce more goods than can be consumed, so the ethic which values work and productivity needs to be replaced, we are told, by an ethic that values leisure and consumption. While the nature of work may change, how one values work and the role of work in one's life is not an open question for the Christian. The Christian values productive activity because the Scripture reveals that work is a part of God's plan for His creation.

God Works

One of the first truths confronting the reader of Scripture is that God works. Indeed, Genesis 1:1 reveals, "In the beginning, God created the heavens and the earth." Also, "by the seventh day God completed His work which He had done" (Gen. 2:2). When God ceased creating, He continued to be active in His creation. The apostle Paul refers to salvation as the good work of God in us which He will continue to perform until the day of Christ Jesus (Phil. 1:6). Christ clearly stated, "My Father is working until now, and I Myself am working" (John 5:17). Indeed, the Scripture, from beginning to end, is a record of the purposeful activity of God, "who works all things after the counsel of His will" (Eph. 1:11).

God is active, and His activity is both purposeful and productive. We who were created in God's image must be impressed by the truth that God works. One of the basic truths of biblical theism is that the Creator is not passive toward His creation but is bringing all things to His appointed conclusion.

In many respects, God's works are different from man's works. God has never been under any constraint to work; He is answerable to no one for His work; His work is predicated by the independent exercise of His good pleasure; His work is always holy; He works without expenditure of effort, time, or resources. Admitting these and other dissimilarities between God's work and man's work, we yet find God Himself comparing the two. In commanding the Sabbath observance, God remarked that man's work week was to follow the pattern of His creative work (Exod. 20:8-11). The creature works because the Creator works.

Adam Worked

When God created Adam in His image, He gave him work to do. After Adam fell into sin, his work took on an entirely different meaning. Sin brought a curse on the ground, resulting in Adam's work becoming toil and labor in the sweat of his face, a constant battle against hindrances to production. But it was not always so. Prior to the advent of sin, Adam had work to do. He was charged with exercising dominion over the garden, naming the animals, being the master of the earth, the subregent under God. Work, then, did not come as a curse on sin; Adam was responsible for purposeful activity prior to his fall into sin.

Biblical Characters and Their Work

Many biblical characters are described by their occupations. We can think of soldiers, shepherds, musicians, homemakers, fishermen, salespersons, farmers, metalworkers, carpenters, and probably many more. Indeed, even God in some of His titles is described by the work that He does. Some of His titles reflect His nature, like Elohim ("God"), or the name Jehovah ("I Am that I Am"). But also, some of His titles are descriptive of His activity on behalf of His people. Examples of these work-oriented titles include "Jehovah-jireh'' (''the Lord will provide''), ''Jehovah-raah'' (''the Lord my shepherd''), and the New Testament ''Kurios'' (''Lord,'' ''Ruler'').

God, who inspired the Bible, did not include such data by accident. The fact that the occupations of so many persons were included in Scripture shows the importance God attaches to the careers of His people. Nothing in our lives is insignificant to Him, and especially is He concerned about His children's careers.

The Fourth Commandment

''Remember the sabbath day, to keep it holy. Six days you shall labor and do all your work'' (Exod. 20:8-9). The wording of this commandment shows that Old Testament believers were commanded to work just as they were commanded to rest. As the Sabbath was to be reminiscent of God's day of rest at the end of the creative week, so the work week was to be a reminder of His work during the creative week. This principle remains important to the New Testament believer who worships on the Lord's Day rather than on the Sabbath, because it shows the high value God attaches to work. This commandment shows that man's work derives from neither the fall into sin nor the Old Testament law, but from the person and work of God Himself. Work's meaning, then, comes from man's creation in God's image, demonstrating through his work patterns his nature as a creature who gains significance from his Creator. Joyce Erickson has stated, ''To a great extent historical understandings of what it means to be human have been closely related to the understanding of the place of work and leisure in human life.''[1]

Laziness

Laziness is never lauded in Scripture. The Book of Proverbs exalts the value of work and rebukes the slothful in such passages as ''In all labor there is profit, but mere talk leads only to poverty'' (Prov. 14:23; see also 18:9; 19:15; 22:29; 24:30-32). In contrasting the faithfulness of servants, Jesus Christ called the unfaithful one a ''wicked and slothful [lazy] slave'' (Matt. 25:26). We get an idea of the seriousness Christ attaches to laziness when He speaks of it as the partner of wickedness.

Leisure and laziness are not synonyms. Proper leisure can be profitable for physical, mental, and spiritual health. In fact, Christ Himself instructed His disciples to make productive use of leisure time (Mark 6:31). But laziness wastes time, thwarts productivity, and generally denies Christ's lordship over life.

---

1. Joyce Erickson. ''Career Education in a Christian Liberal Arts Setting: Some Preliminary Consideration.'' *Christian Scholar's Review* 6. No. 2 (1976):169.

No Work, No Food

When Paul wrote to the church at Thessalonica, one of the problems he addressed was laziness. Evidently, some church members there were refusing to work, and then expecting other members to support them. Paul called such parasitic living "unruly" behavior, and he directed, "If anyone will not work, neither let him eat" (II Thess. 3:10). Paul's order did not apply to those who could not work, but only to those who refused to work.

Some believers at Thessalonica were evidently confused about the Lord's return, using the concept of His imminent return as an excuse for laziness. Pious as it might have sounded, Paul rejected it and cited his own example of hard work (probably making tents) as a pattern of godly living. Paul labelled those who refused to work as "unruly," "undisciplined," "disobedient," and "busybodies." He considered their irresponsibility so serious that he instructed other Christians to avoid them (II Thess. 3:6). Responsible Christian living, on the other hand, includes a self-respect that results in productive work.

Some Implications

One implication from the Bible's teaching on work is that there is a reciprocal relationship between our work and our identity. Such identification was neither accidental nor meaningless. Our careers usually grow out of our sense of identity, and at the same time, they help determine our identities. For this reason, a proper self-concept is vitally important in the selection of one's career. The correlation between identity and career is evident not only in Scripture but also in our behavior patterns. When asked to tell who we are, few of us speak very long before mentioning our careers, or our plans for a future career. In that sense, we are identifying ourselves by our careers. For the same reason, many persons experience a severe identity crisis at retirement. Up to that time, much of the retiree's identity was determined by his career, and when that career is finished, an identity vacuum exists until something else is found to fill the void. Earlier in one's work life, if one suddenly finds himself out of work, the economic deprivation is often overshadowed by the ensuing identity crisis. Still earlier, when a teenager speaks of selecting a career, he says "I'm trying to decide what to *be.*" One's sense of identity is shown to be vitally connected with his career in such statements as "I'm going to *be* a teacher," rather than, "I plan to find employment in education." Many women are experiencing identity crises because their activities at work or home do not coincide with the persons they think they are or want to be. A career, then is not merely incidental to the Christian's life, since it is intricately connected to this identity. It does matter what work we do, because what we do may affect what we think about ourselves. And the opposite is also true—what we think about ourselves influences what we choose to do vocationally and how well we do it.

A second implication is that a believer's career should mean much more to him than merely a means of supporting himself in order to spread the gospel. At first glance, Paul appears to have engaged in tent-making only to pay the bills for evangelism, but in actual fact it was much more than that. He used this "secular" work itself to teach vital spiritual truths (II Thess. 3). The "secular" work, in other words, had "spiritual" value in and of itself. There is a view abroad in Christendom that if one has a career in business, education, government, or anything other than a Christian service vocation, then his career is substandard, and only a means of earning a livelihood while spreading the gospel. While recognizing our responsibility to spread the gospel, we must realize that this view does great violence to the biblical meaning of work. A career must be more than a "necessary evil" for the believer if he is to think of his work as God thinks of it. God's leadership constitutes a career as "sacred," no matter what that career is. This notion obviously challenges the hierarchical theory that some God-given work is of higher status before God than other work, that "full-time Christian service" is a higher calling of God than His other calls. While not demeaning Christian service careers in the least, we need to acknowledge that whatever call God issues, He does so as it pleases Him and for His glory. The "sacredness" of a career depends not upon the work itself, but upon the spirituality of the worker.

A third implication follows from the orderliness and purposefulness of God, namely, that God has a plan for the life of every believer. While this plan includes every facet of life—more than the career alone—it certainly includes the believer's career. Proper stewardship of life itself demands discovering and doing God's plan.

A fourth implication comes from the importance of the believer's life in God's sight. Work is important, not only for its impact on identity and its relationship to obedience, but also because it consumes a significant portion of time. Those who accept the challenge to make every part of life count for God's glory (I Cor. 10:31), and to do all things in the name of the Lord Jesus (Col. 3:17), surely must view their work with a deep sense of its importance. Paul was speaking to slaves, who might be most tempted to think of their work as unimportant, when he said, "Whatever you do, do your work heartily as for the Lord rather than for men" (Col. 3:23). No believer's work is trivial, no matter what it is, when the believer is fulfilling God's calling and working for God's glory. When viewed in the light of this value, even the most menial task can be seen to have eternal significance. And when we are working for God's glory, this reminds us that the work is not an end in itself; it does not become an idol. We can appreciate its value in our lives and in His kingdom while rejecting the temptation to become "workaholics."

Conclusion

Work is important because the Creator built it into His creation. Consequently, an acceptance of the vital function of a career is essential to a believer's stewardship of his life. Some may ridicule what they call an "antiquated Puritan work ethic" because of the plentitude of goods in an industrialized world. But the believer values work because his values are deeper than the values of those who work only out of economic necessity. The Christian's values are based on God's revelation rather than on technological innovations.

QUESTIONS FOR A PERSONAL INVENTORY

1. How do you view work? Is it a necessary evil, or a source of enjoyment? Circle the number on the scale that represents your present viewpoint.

Hate Work		Necessary Evil			Necessary		Love Work		
1	2	3	4	5	6	7	8	9	10

2. Suppose you recently inherited five million dollars. Since you would not *have* to work, how would you spend your time?

3. Analyze your answer to question 2. What does it tell you about your values toward work? toward money? toward leisure?

work:

money:

leisure:

4. What goals have you set for yourself in the past month for any area of your life? In how many of these are you showing progress?

3 *Elements of the Lord's Will*

One of the chief problems in the search for "the Lord's will" is that we usually do not know what we are looking for. In most cases, we probably already know the Lord's will but have not recognized it for what it is. Or we already have the necessary information, but we do not know how to coordinate it into a knowledge of His plan.

What Is "the Lord's Will"?

When the Scriptures speak about "God's will," only rarely do they use the term to refer to God's plan for Christians' careers. Although various words are translated "will" in the Scripture, when used of God, they have in common the concept of His volition, or choice, and usually are an expression of His eternal purpose for Himself or for His creation. God's will is His faculty of determining what *should* and what *will* come to pass.

The *should* and the *will* point us to two aspects of God's will which deserve consideration, and the Bible seems to present two overlapping but somewhat distinct concepts.[1] First, God determines what comes to pass, and this aspect of His will is referred to as His *determined* will, or decrees. This aspect of God's will is inevitable, having been established in eternity past. There is nothing in which He is not sovereignly involved, for His unchanging plan comprehends the world in general and our lives in particular. Passages such as Ephesians 1:3-14 and Romans 9 amply teach and illustrate this decretive aspect of God's will. God's decrees usually are known only in retrospect, as we view in enlightened hindsight how He has already worked.

A second manner in which the Scripture refers to God's will points to His *desires,* or His prescriptions for us. God prescribes certain standards of behavior, for instance, and is pleased when we fulfill these expectations. And in making such desires known to us, He is placing responsibility on us for obedience. It is His command, for example, that husbands love their

---

1. J. Grant Howard. *Knowing God's Will and Doing It!* (Grand Rapids, Mich.: Zondervan Pub. Co., 1976), pp. 11ff.

wives as Christ loved the church (Eph. 4:25), but He has not decreed that love absolutely certain. In fact, there are many husbands who do not love their wives, and who will be held accountable by God for their disobedience to this command.

Whether our careers are in God's determined will or desired will is probably impossible to decide, for the overlap between these two aspects of God's will is considerable. God's sovereignty surely encompasses the distribution of talents, spiritual gifts, experiences, and interests that are involved in vocational decisions. And yet, there seems to be a responsibility placed on each of us for the discovery, development, and faithful use of our talents, gifts, and interests. How our apparently free choices are exercised within the context of God's ultimate sovereignty remains one of the mysteries of Christian theology. Generally, we will approach the topic of God's will in vocational matters by emphasizing our responsibility and obedience, for stewardship of life appears to be an area of God's will that we can know and should fulfill.

The Scripture reveals that the will of God includes our salvation: "It is not the will of our Father who is in heaven that one of these little ones perish" (Matt. 18:14). "He predestinated us to adoption as sons through Jesus Christ to Himself, according to the kind intention of His will" (Eph. 1:5). Paul clearly says that God's will is the ultimate basis of salvation.

God's will is very frequently referred to as the basis and direction for Christian living. The apostle Paul assumed that when one had the Scriptures, he had the information necessary to know God's will (Rom. 2:18). And God has filled Scripture with indications of His will for our Christian living. For instance, I Peter 4:2 states that the believer should "live the rest of the time in the flesh no longer for the lusts of men, but for the will of God." In that same Epistle, Peter gave directions for relating to government authority, and then said, "for such is the will of God" (I Pet. 2:15). Paul became very specific regarding one aspect of Christian behavior, saying, "This is the will of God, your sanctification; that is, that you abstain from sexual immorality" (I Thess. 4:3). In Colossians 1:9-10, Paul prayed that the Christians would be "filled with the knowledge of His will in all spiritual wisdom and understanding, so that you may walk in a manner worthy of the Lord, to please Him in all respects. . . ."

Clearly, in the vast majority of Scripture passages that speak about God's will for us, that will concerns our salvation and Christian character.

In only a few cases, Scripture speaks about the Lord's will in a career context. Paul stated on several occasions that he was an apostle "by the will of God" (I Cor. 1:1; II Cor. 1:1; Eph. 1:1; Col. 1:1; II Tim. 1:1). Also, though he did not use the word "will," in other instances he said that his apostleship came by God's commandment or God's call, which are expressions of God's purpose. As he discharged his calling as an apostle, he spoke of the will of God in regard to his travels (Rom. 1:10; 15:32). And James instructs us to set our goals in business with a realization of God's overriding sovereignty, so that we say, "If the Lord wills, we shall live and do this or that" (James 4:15).

God's Will for Persons

From the discussions above, it is evident that the scriptural emphasis in speaking of God's will for an individual focuses on his salvation and personal qualities. This priority cannot be overemphasized. God's will for His children centers on the quality of people we are, not merely on our vocations.

At first glance, this scriptural emphasis may appear to treat the Christian's vocation as insignificant. In actual fact, however, it shows the importance of godly attitudes and behavior in all major life decisions.

The person who is seeking to fulfill God's will for his personal life will be better equipped to discern God's will regarding his vocation than he would be if he were rebelling against God. Prayer and Bible study make our hearts more sensitive to the leadership of the Lord, with the result that we have an increased ability to recognize God's will when He makes it known. A conscious effort to live obediently, as children of God, gives credibility to our requests for a knowledge of God's will for a specific decision.

When we are living in God's will for our personal lives, we will be diligently working at what God has already shown us to be His will. A frequently encountered pitfall is the trap of inactivity, which often works in the following manner. One who is genuinely concerned about God's will for his future may allow this concern to dominate him to the extent that he does not adequately fulfill God's will for the present. For instance, many students who want to know God's will for them after graduation become so involved with this concern that they neglect to study. They neglect God's will on a daily basis, hoping at the same time to discover it on a long-range basis. On the other hand, the student who realizes that God's will for him on a daily basis includes responsible and diligent study will have a much more receptive attitude and spiritual understanding toward God's will for his life after graduation. Similarly, the adult who wishes to know God's will about changing jobs should not be negligent in his current position, but should work to his highest capacity.

One business executive told me that he was searching for God's will in a career change. He had lost interest in his current job to the extent that he was functioning at a substandard level and had placed himself in real jeopardy regarding that job. He was neglecting God's will for his present situation since he was not doing the work God had already given him to do to the best of his ability. Not only was this neglect harmful to him, but it also caused his fellow workers to think less of him and his Christian testimony. Once this executive began performing again to the best of his ability, he began to discern God's plan for his future. Being faithful to the Lord in his present situation was the best preparation he could make for his future. He changed jobs soon after this growth occurred in his Christian life, and at last report, was thoroughly enjoying his new work and was a credit to his company.

Several basic principles are operative in this concentration on daily living. First, we acknowledge that God's will for us is for us as persons, not merely as vocational units of production. To limit "God's will" to vocation is to distort the meaning of work for the Christian; it implies that His interest is not in us as persons but only as components in an impersonal cosmic scheme. Second, we also acknowledge God's sovereignty in placing us in our current situation. To act irresponsibly toward our current duties would be to show a low opinion of God's will for us currently. What better example of hypocrisy can we think of than this: disregarding God's will for the present, while seeking to know it for the future. Third, we demonstrate an understanding that the Christian life is not an assortment of occasional spurts of commitment, but is a life of daily walking with the Lord. Knowing God's will, likewise, is not an occasional or infrequent concern, but is a priority in daily Christian living. Finally, we avoid worry over God's will for our future when we concentrate on daily obedience. When Christ taught His disciples about worry (Matt. 6:25 ff.), He showed that worry focused on the future, with the usual accompaniment of inactivity in the present. Christ concluded by stating, "Each day has enough trouble of its own" (Matt. 6:34). By focusing our attention and effort on today's challenges, opportunities, and problems, we avoid the sin of worry, and we are better equipped to face tomorrow's challenges when they arrive tomorrow.

Since the Lord's will, in Scripture, centers so frequently on our personal lives, the cultivation of practical godliness in daily living is of primary importance in living the God-planned life. In addition to Bible study and prayer, a conscious effort at obedience and submission is essential in producing persons who truly desire God's will. To concentrate on being the kind of people God wants us to be is to take the most important step in discovering His will for individual decisions in our lives.

23

God's Plan in God's Word

God's written Word, the authoritative guide for Christian living, is vitally important in the career decision. Frequently, however, we fail to use the Word because we simply do not know how to use it.

A common misuse of the Word is to ignore it altogether in the career decision. Many believers have followed the advice, "Just pray, and do what you feel the Lord is leading you to do." In other words, "Ask God for guidance, then follow your feelings." This advice seriously confuses "feeling" with "thinking," and the result is usually an emotionally based decision that ignores God's Word. Such an approach misuses the Word by thinking of it as a mystical force influencing life without significant mental activity. God's Word changes lives by changing thinking, and its power is most keenly felt in the lives of those who understand it. One can be the person God wants him to be only by following what he *knows* from Scripture, not merely following what he *feels* after prayer.

Another common misuse of Scripture, the other extreme, is a compulsion to find a specific verse as the basis for one's call into a vocation. Most Christians have no doubt heard testimonies of how God directed someone to the mission field (or to some other vocation) through a particular verse of Scripture. While God may use such a method to guide some believers, serious problems result when we assume He must always use that means. To use missions as an example, we can see how God may use Scripture verses dealing with evangelism to impress a Christian with the necessity and rewards of serving as a missionary. But how would God use this method to lead a believer into accounting, or plumbing, or sales, or any number of other careers? Believers who feel intimidated because they do not have a specific verse to which they can attach their careers frequently make one of two mistakes. They may conclude that the Scripture has nothing to do with their careers, and that their vocations are consequently inferior to those to which Scripture is more closely related. The second mistake may be to wrest a verse from its context and obvious meaning to make it apply to a specific career. Both errors show an essentially low view of Scripture by limiting its applicability.

How, then, can we use the Scripture correctly in making a career decision?

First, we can recognize the great amount of information contained in Scripture to direct our personal lives—our attitudes, behaviors, values, etc. Since God's will concerns primarily the kind of people we are, we need to submit ourselves continually and consciously to the authority of God's word in forming our attitudes and selecting our behaviors. Since it is God's will, for instance, for a husband to love his wife (Eph. 5:25), a husband can

24

concentrate on being as loving as possible to his wife, and thus be fulfilling God's will. To rebel against this portion of God's will, while asking God to reveal more of His will, would be presumptuous indeed.

Likewise, it is God's will for children to obey their parents, to honor both father and mother (Eph. 6:1-3). It would be absurd for a high school student to request a knowledge of God's will for a future career while rebelling against his parents, and thereby refusing God's will for the present. Submission to the Scriptures will enable us to grow into the persons God wants us to be, which is basic to doing what He wants us to do. Since the Bible is filled with specific instructions for our personal lives, we have a reliable guide in our effort to be the persons God wants each of us to be.

Second, the Word of God provides a basis for our sense of personal identity, and that identity greatly influences our career decisions. The Scriptures teach that our existence and function on earth are neither accidental nor meaningless, but rather the expression of the sovereign purpose of God. The God who gives meaning to life does have a plan for His children, each of whom receives significance because of his relationship to the Father. To have a biblically based self-esteem is to avoid both sinful extremes of pride and undue debasement, and it further involves a realistic appraisal of our talents and limitations. Since our careers are closely related to our sense of identity, the influence that the Word of God has on our sense of identity is crucial in the career decision.

Third, the Scripture should provide the base of our value systems. What is important to me? What is more important, what less important? The answers to these questions show our values, which hopefully are based upon the Word of God and operating on a conscious level in our decisions. As a simple example, a Christian might decide to turn down a highly paying position because it would require him to misrepresent a product or service. In such a case, the value of honesty is of greater importance than the value of money. Or another person may accept a promotion, even though it means moving away from established friends, because his value of achievement is greater than his value of those particular acquaintances.

The Bible speaks very directly to moral issues (such as lying, stealing, etc.) and should mold our values on these issues. As Christians we will not, hopefully, make a career decision to engage in a practice clearly condemned in God's Word. But in addition, we should allow the Scripture to form our values toward such life areas as the role of our church, family, friends, or job. The Bible should also guide our values toward money, leisure, advancement, competition, lifestyle, recognition, commitment to a task, authority, and probably many other career-oriented concerns. In actual fact, we all

25

have values in these areas; it is quite probable that they have been formed by influences other than God's Word and that they operate without our awareness of them. A helpful exercise for the serious Christian is to examine several recent decisions to see what values were really operating, and then examine those values in the light of Scripture.

Clearly, the written Word of God can have a decisive roll in career decisions, as it should in all decisions. In some cases, God may use it to speak directly to the decision; in most cases, God uses it to mold the person who decides.

The Persons God Has Made Us

Since God is both orderly and personal, He does not exercise His lordship in a chaotic or aimless fashion. We would expect, therefore, to gain insight into His plan for our future lives by examining how He has already worked in our lives. God does not bring interests, experiences, abilities, or limitations into our lives capriciously, but rather, purposefully. Consequently, an examination of ourselves and our past experiences can bring genuine insight into God's plan. For instance, probably no New Testament character was more radically changed during his life than was the apostle Paul. Yet, a closer examination shows that even experiences and education *prior to his salvation* were used by God in his later ministry. Seeing his ministry, we can appreciate how God used even his early life in shaping him.

Consequently, to say that God is orderly is not to encourage a speculating contest, trying to second-guess God's moves. It is, however, an acknowledgment that His leading will not be antithetical to the way He has already worked in our lives.

Since our interests, abilities, experiences, and personality factors are given to us purposefully by the One whose plan we are trying to discern, we should carefully examine ourselves to see how God has already worked in our lives. The following chapter deals with examination in depth, and so further explanation need not be made at this point.

The Opportunities God Gives Us

God, who is Lord of the universe as well as Lord of individual lives, is sovereign in placing opportunities before His children. His sovereignty must be acknowledged in the fact that some persons are born into cultures and political systems that limit educational and career opportunities, while others are born into societies with wide opportunities. Even in comparatively free nations, however, some seem to have more opportunities than others due to socio-economic status, condition of health, abilities, race, family background, and numerous other factors. While admitting that such differences exist (sometimes, apparently unjustly), a common problem is that we do not recognize the opportunities we have, or we do not act responsibly toward those opportunities.

As we need to know the persons God has made us, so we need to know the opportunities He gives us. One who creatively combines his interests, abilities, and desires into a career goal is usually able to search out and pursue educational and career possibilities that may not be readily apparent to others. While God gives opportunities, He likewise expects responsible action on the part of His children.

While we begin to accumulate information about ourselves, therefore, we can also be acquiring a knowledge of various occupations. Occupations normally require certain abilities, interests, and personality traits, and as we discover or develop qualities in these facets of life, we can investigate occupations that capitalize on the qualities we possess.

God can lead us in spite of our ignorance, but He never prizes ignorance. The Christian who seriously desires to know God's plan will not sit passively, waiting for a supernatural disclosure, but will diligently pursue all sources of information God has already provided.

It is truly astounding to realize that many people choose college majors or jobs without any idea what those majors or jobs will involve. Although they may claim a mystical "leading" from the Lord, they are usually the first to become disillusioned and drop out from school or quit their jobs. That type of blind decision-making shows a low estimation of one's stewardship of life from the Lord. Chapter 5 will deal with important factors regarding opportunities to be considered in a Christian's career decision.

God's Plan as a Process

Does God's will for a Christian's vocation ever change? Frequently, one is criticized if he professes being led by the Lord into a vocation, and then led into something else a few years later. A successful pastor once told me, "I think God is leading me from the pastorate to some other service. In fact, I've thought this for a couple of years. But I've been afraid to make the move, because my family would think I'm turning my back on God's will." Had God changed His mind? Had this pastor missed God's will?

The Scripture abounds with evidence that God works according to His purpose which He established in eternity past. His plans are not contingent upon human whims, nor does He change His mind (Eph. 1:4, 11; Mal. 3:6; James 1:17). Yet at the same time, He normally does not choose to reveal His entire plan for our lives at any one time, but rather leads us a step at a time in the life of faith. Consequently, as one stage after another is unveiled, it may appear as if God has changed His mind, while in reality, His overall plan has not changed at all.

To say that God's plan is set does not mean that it is static. The fact that God's plan for one's life includes working as a salesman, for instance, does not mean that God's plan is for that person always to be a salesman. His plan may include a promotion to sales manager, or to some other business position, or to some position completely outside the business realm. An appropriate biblical example of this truth is David. At one point in David's life God's will for him was to be a shepherd, but he did not remain a shepherd all his life. Later, God's will for him was to serve as a musician, then as a warrior, and later as a king. God's will did not change—He knew all along what He was doing—but God unfolded it to David a step at a time.

Of particular sensitivity in the Christian community is this principle when applied to those in Christian service careers. We tend to think that those called to the pastorate or to missions have a lifelong calling. To leave that calling for another often causes confusion and criticism. While many do consider their calling a lifetime commitment, there does not seem to be New Testament proof either way. God may have a specific function for one to fulfill in a particular ministry, and then another function in another ministry. In fact, Christ taught us to expect that type of mobility, for He taught that when we are faithful in few things we are made master over many things (Matt. 25:21, 23).

Discovery of God's Will—A Spiritual Process

To this point, it may seem as if the Lord's will is discovered in a very mechanical, analytical manner. To a great degree, it is. Many Christians operate on the misconception that for something to be spiritual, it must be largely *emotional*. Consequently, any process involving careful and methodical thinking is suspected as the "thoughts of man" rather than the "wisdom of God."

As the term "spiritual" is used in Scripture describing believers, it carries the idea of being controlled by the Holy Spirit, with all the resultant blessings. The word "spiritual" itself shows us how this control is exercised: the emphasis is on man's thinking and understanding rather than on his emotions. A good illustration is Colossians 1:9: ". . . we have not ceased to pray for you and to ask that you may be filled with the knowledge of His will in all spiritual wisdom and understanding." A spiritual experience, then, is not essentially a mystical process or an emotional upheaval; it is a walk with God in the knowledge of His Word.

28

As we seek to discover God's will, we need to rely continually on God's grace. When we investigate ourselves and analyze potential vocations, we run the danger of adopting the attitude that we deserve God's leadership or that we merit a particular outcome. But neither ''deserve'' nor ''merit'' are in the vocabulary of grace. Our attitude must be one of humble reliance on God for insight into His will, and for strength to accomplish it. When we are living correctly in His will, we will give praise and glory to God for everything.

Neither should our concern for investigations and analyses lead to the conclusion that prayer is unnecessary. When Jesus taught His disciples to pray, His model prayer included the petition, ''Thy will be done on earth as it is in heaven'' (Matt. 6:10). The Christian has no better way of demonstrating his reliance on God than through prayer. In prayer we approach His ''throne of grace, that we may receive mercy and may find grace to help in time of need'' (Heb. 4:16). If prayer is considered inconsistent with responsible analysis and thinking, then there must be a serious distortion of one's view of prayer. We do not pray in order to be relieved of the use of the rational faculties God gives us. Rather, we pray for God's mercy and grace so that we may use our sin-affected minds correctly.

In fact, if thoughtful inquiry is not conducted, we cannot truly pray for wisdom in our decisions. The Lord through His apostle encourages us in that ''if any of you lacks wisdom, let him ask of God, who gives to all men generously and without reproach, and it will be given to him'' (James 1:5). Too often, however, we may pray for wisdom without knowing what we are requesting. We may think that *wisdom* is some God-given insight which makes research and knowledge unnecessary, and so we may ask for it thinking that it will be a short cut to a decision. The problem with this thinking, however, is that it ignores the meaning of the word ''wisdom.'' While *wisdom* surely is a broader word than *knowledge,* it does not operate without knowledge. *Wisdom* includes mental excellence used in a manner that results in genuine goodness.[2] Spiritual *wisdom,* then, is neither an escape from knowledge nor a shortcut around mental activity. When we pray for wisdom, therefore, we are assuming the responsibility of acquiring appropriate knowledge, and we are asking God for the ability to assign proper significance to that knowledge and use it to make a good decision.

The more we rely on God's grace, are controlled by His Spirit, and are frequently, prayerfully in His Word, the more our minds will be renewed to understand God, ourselves, and His will for our lives.

---

2. R. C. Trench. *Synonyms of the New Testament* (Grand Rapids: Wm. B. Eerdmans Pub. Co., 1953), p. 283.

Summary

The primary focus of God's will for our lives is on our total lives as redeemed persons, not merely on our vocational choice. When the quality of our daily living is that which fulfills His revealed will, we will be spiritually prepared to make decisions that correspond to His plan for us. God's Word is absolutely essential, for through it God develops our knowledge of Him, our values, and our insight into ourselves, thus directing our decision. Thoughtful evaluation of the previous work of God in our lives and the opportunities He gives us is an integral part of discerning His unfolding plan for us. Since this discovery is a spiritual (i.e., Spirit-directed) process, prayer for God's leadership and wisdom is imperative. The spiritual person is one who walks with God, not merely during crisis or decision times, but consistently and knowledgeably.

QUESTIONS FOR PERSONAL INVENTORY

1. What values or concerns have you used in making your career choices up to now? On what biblical principles are these values based?

VALUES	BIBLICAL PRINCIPLE
example: helping others	example: ministry, kindness (Eph.4:32; Col.5:12; I Pet.3:8-9)
1.	1.
2.	2.
3.	3.
4.	4.

2. What careers can you definitely *eliminate* from consideration because they would cause you to *violate* some biblical principle?

CAREERS	BIBLICAL PRINCIPLE
example: bartender	example: drunkenness
	(Prov. 23:21; Hab. 2:15)
1.	1.
2.	2.
3.	3.
4.	4.

3. What experiences did the apostle Paul have *prior to his salvation* that were used in his calling as an apostle? (You may need to review the book of Acts.)

1.

2.

3.

4.

4 *The Person God Has Made*

God did not arrive at His plans for our lives by generating in computer fashion a list of random alternatives, and then assigning them arbitrarily to us. He is both orderly and personal. Not only is His will from eternity, but Scripture also indicates that He begins working in our lives from the moment of conception (Jer. 1:4-5; Rom 9:10-13). Consequently, we can gain insight into what God expects from us by analyzing what He has already done in us.

Self-discovery can be threatening. It is often easier to learn about ourselves than it is to accept what we learn. Scripture warns against two extremes in self-acceptance in Romans 12:3:

> For through the grace given to me I say to every man among you not to think of himself more highly than he ought to think; but to think so as to have sound judgment, as God has allotted to each a measure of faith.

First, we are warned against self-exaggeration, or pride. Our self-discovery should not lead us to attach more importance to ourselves than we deserve. We probably all know individuals who have become so fascinated with themselves—their talents, personality, experiences—that they overlook others' talents as well as their own limitations. We are all subject to the sin of pride.

Next, the Scripture cautions us against self-depreciation, admonishing us to recognize that we each have "a measure of faith." Succeeding verses connect this "measure of faith" with specific gifts and encourage us to exercise our gifts within the body of Christ. The self-depreciating person usually belittles himself, his abilities, his experiences. This defeatist syndrome actually denies God's Word by refusing to acknowledge that the Lord has worked in the Christian's life. Often mistakenly equated with humility, this self-depreciation affects many of us.

The proper balance between the extremes of self-exaggeration and self-depreciation is illustrated by the apostle Paul's statement, "By the grace of God, I am what I am" (I Cor. 15:10). By not denying anything God had done, through, or for him, Paul avoided self-depreciation. But at the same time, he acknowledged that whatever benefits he enjoyed were from God's grace, and so he also refrained from the sin of self-exaggeration.

As we discover what the orderly, personal God has placed in our lives, we will also become aware of some pronounced deficiencies or limitations. God has not given any of us all possible talents, or all interests, or all experiences, and we should be thankful that He has not. With each talent comes responsibility, and if we had only gifts without limitations, our responsibilities would be unbearable. But sometimes, when we discover a limitation, we fixate on that to the point that we overlook numerous talents. Limitations can be just as helpful in discerning God's plan as are abilities, if we determine to use them productively.

The remainder of this chapter will help us focus on different aspects of our lives in an effort to discover what God has already done in us. While other factors may be crucial to some persons, the following topics usually are a guide to self-discovery sufficient for career decision-making.

Abilities and Limitations

As believers, we must acknowledge that our abilities did not come to us arbitrarily or randomly, but were invested in our lives by the sovereign, personal God. Since God's works are purposeful, we should carefully examine our abilities to see how they enlighten us regarding God's plan for our careers.

As with interests, abilities may appear in almost all life experiences. School experiences, both classes and extracurricular activities, are helpful in highlighting abilities and limitations. A young person who is active in many types of activities usually has a good background of experiences by which to judge his abilities.

Ability requires cultivation and practice; it does not simply emerge. Consequently, a responsibility rests upon us as Christians to attempt to develop any abilities we think we may have. In the parable of the talents (Matt. 25:14-30), Christ spoke of the Christian's responsibility to use his abilities. The two servants who used their talents were blessed, while the one who failed to cultivate his was condemned as both wicked and lazy. The talents invested in our lives are not ours to possess, but ours to develop and to use as stewards for God.

One of the most frequently examined abilities is mental ability, or intelligence. Many students and adults alike think that an I.Q. (intelligence quotient) test can tell them all they need to know about their mental abilities in order to plan their lives. Actually, there are a number of I.Q. tests available, each somewhat different from the rest, and so the meaning of an

I.Q. score depends upon which test was used. The practical value of I.Q. scores has been questioned by many researchers who doubt the tests' ability to measure raw mental ability (i.e., ability as distinct from achievement, environmental influences, etc.). The I.Q. may still have some value, but it is dangerous to assume that one's level of intelligence is the only factor to be considered in a career decision.

In reality, there are many types of mental abilities, some of which cannot be tested or shown in classroom learning situations. Recognizing the distinction of *types* (as opposed to *levels)* of mental ability can be encouraging to individuals who may think they have no future because of poor classroom performance. Many students (and their parents) have become distressed when told, ''You are not college material,'' thinking that the mental ability demanded for college learning was the only important type of intelligence. Since they thought only of intelligence *levels,* they thought the future was bleak. A recognition of intelligence *types,* however, has prompted many to begin a productive search to uncover their own mental abilities.

Following are a number of mental abilities which both expand and deviate from the stereotyped view of I.Q., but which should be considered in assessing strengths and weaknesses.[1]

Verbal Abilities

> Writing understandably
> Conversing and relating informally
> Speaking to an audience
> Persuading others
> Negotiating to an agreement
> Knowing several languages

Numerical Abilities

> Computing quickly and accurately
> Seeing quantitative relationships
> Solving quantitative problems

Social Abilities

> Dealing with different types of people
> Relating easily in social situations
> Dressing and grooming presentably
> Dealing with criticism

---

1. Adapted from Howard E. Figler, *PATH: A Career Workbook for Liberal Arts Students* (Cranston, R.I.: Carroll Press, 1975), pp. 95-97.

Investigative Abilities

> Inquiring into scientific phenomena
> Gathering information systematically
> Recognizing relationships among data

Manual/Physical Abilities

> Understanding the way machines operate
> Recognizing relationships among mechanical operations
> Visualizing spatial relationships
> Using hands and/or body with skill and strength
> Resisting physical fatigue

Creative Abilities

> Creating new ideas and forms with physical objects
> Sensing aesthetic values
> Imagining new relationships in ideas, programs, behavior, objects, etc.

Instructional Abilities

> Helping others to learn or understand
> Clarifying or simplifying abstract ideas or relationships
> Counseling and other similar helping relationships

Managerial Abilities

> Directing others in work
> Organizing and planning systematically
> Coordinating resources
> Recognizing and making decisions
> Handling details
> Arranging information in an orderly fashion
> Pursuing a task until completion

We have probably all known individuals whom we consider brilliant, but who had little or no "common sense." Or perhaps we know a top language student who could not pass mechanical drafting, or a competent physician who would be totally unable to repair his automobile. These are all examples of the principle that mental ability must be considered in terms of *types* as well as *levels*.

Since God is orderly, we must conclude that He entrusts us with abilities for a purpose. And since He is personal, His distribution of abilities reflects

His personal concern for us as individuals. Consequently, our abilities give good indication of God's plan for our lives. Of course, we may have abilities that we use outside vocation (in hobbies or in volunteer work), but the existence of abilities should at least prompt investigation of vocational applications. And since these abilities are God-given, their values are spiritually equivalent as far as the Christian is concerned. The ability to repair automobiles or washing machines is as important and as sacred as the ability to teach a class or to manage a bank. God gives abilities according to His good pleasure and for our benefit, and so whatever ability He gives can be used for His glory and our fulfillment.

Assessment of ability is difficult, and reliable aptitude tests are limited. But as Christians, we are not limited to psychological or physiological tests to discover our abilities. We can prayerfully examine our experiences to see if competencies are shown in our performance. Experiences in different school courses often reveal abilities and limitations, as do experiences in extracurricular clubs and activities. Consequently, taking a wide variety of courses and participating in several different extracurricular activities can give good experience for career choice. Active participation in a local church puts one in numerous situations that might reveal competencies (real or potential) in numerous areas, including teaching, preaching, music, management, accounting, human relations, leadership, organization, helping, and recreation. In addition, the New Testament records that our fellow-believers can be helpful in recognizing our abilities (Acts 13:2; I Tim. 4:14). Godly persons within the local church who are known for their spiritual discernment often recognize ability in others within that fellowship.

None of our abilities came to us by accident. Since God has given specific abilities to each of us, we should do what we can to discover and develop them; they could definitely point us to His plan for our careers.

Interests

God does not develop interests in our lives capriciously, and therefore, our interests can be very helpful in making career decisions. Interest patterns tend to emerge from our total life experiences, and by later adolescence, many people have very pronounced vocational interests.

Unfortunately, God is not the only one who prompts interests. The believer needs to be extremely careful to examine his interests by the standard of Scripture, to make certain that his interests do not violate any clear teaching of the Word.

Interests often develop through school experiences, and that is one reason for students to expose themselves to as many fields of study as possible, thus giving good opportunity for interests to emerge. Often, interests surface in school extracurricular activities (clubs, band, athletics, newspaper, plays, etc.), church functions, hobbies, community functions, and any number of other activities. Wide reading usually fosters interests, as does exposure to a variety of interesting people in various vocations. Parents' interests frequently influence children's interests, with the children then entering their parents' professions. Also, an admired adult (such as a teacher) often arouses vocational interest in an adolescent because he identifies with that adult.

As interests can arise from almost all life experiences, so can dislikes (noninterests). Exposure to experiences and fields of study usually results in some aversions as well as some attractions. This should be expected, and welcomed, since it too can be a means to focusing on God's plan.

Vocational interest tests are readily available that measure an individual's interests usually by comparing his interests to those of persons who have succeeded in various professions. Two of the more popular tests are the *Strong-Campbell Interest Inventory*[2] and the *Kuder Occupational Interest Survey*.[3] The *Strong-Campbell* test further profiles a person's interests according to the personality-interest themes developed by J. L. Holland (realistic, conventional, enterprising, investigative, artistic, social).[4] Such data can be helpful to the Christian, but obviously should not be the sole basis of his decision regarding a career.

An important question to ask about our interests is the following: "What is it, specifically, about this field that interests me?" It may very well be that the interest is real but is not sufficiently broad or intense enough to consider it as a career. For example, one may have an active interest in woodworking, frequently using a home workshop. That person may not, however, have the type of interest that would be required to work as a carpenter, all day every day. Another person might have an active interest in his own investments, but would not be interested in the pressure of managing other people's investments as a career.

A common source of professional frustration is the mistake of thinking about vocational interests in a stereotyped manner. This occurs when one thinks his interests dictate either "vocation A" or "vocation B." Instead, if we carefully evaluate our interests (and other factors), we can creatively combine the specific aspects that appeal to us from various vocations, and

---

2. David P. Campbell, *Strong-Campbell Interest Inventory* (Stanford: Stanford University Press, 1974).

3. G. Frederick Kuder, *Occupational Interest Survey* (Chicago: Science Research Associates, 1971).

4. J. L. Holland, *Making Vocational Choices: A Theory of Careers* (Prentice-Hall, 1973).

aim at a more satisfying career target. For instance, a student may enjoy both psychology and business courses, but may not wish to pursue either of them totally for his career. He may be able to combine what he likes from both fields, however, into a fulfilling career in personnel management, industrial psychology, market research, or a variety of other alternatives.

In a rapidly changing, technological society, many college students enter jobs at graduation that did not even exist when they were freshmen. This condition allows those in the job market to combine their interests creatively into rewarding careers. Since the Christian is to do all things heartily and as unto the Lord, believers ought to examine themselves and their career alternatives if they feel trapped in jobs in which they have little interest.

Personality Traits

It is well known that personality is influenced by an almost infinite variety of experiences in life, actually beginning prior to birth. This has led many to the conclusion that as persons, we are helpless and at the mercy of our heredity and our environment, which form our personalities.

While admitting the influence of both heredity and environment on personality, the Christian does not believe that they are the ultimate causes of personality. Rather, our life experiences (interacting with our environment) are directed by our loving Heavenly Father, working them together for our good (Rom. 8:28). Our personalities, therefore, need to be seen as evidence of God's work in our lives.

Of course, some personality traits are neither good nor godly (such as anxiety, bitterness, irresponsibility, depressions, etc.). But as we examine our personality traits, those that do not violate God's Word can be indicative of His will for life.

Some persons, for instance, are "self-starters," people with new ideas and abundant enthusiasm. That trait combination might be more effective in public relations work than might an equally intelligent person who is shy and retiring. Neither extreme is morally good or bad in itself, but both need to be considered in selection of a career goal. Similarly, different vocations require different levels of independence, patience, flexibility, and rewards. Also, some careers involve prolonged pressure or tension, hazardous risk-taking, or frequent mobility. Some require frequent contact with other people, while some involve contact only with machines. Still others require constant manipulation of ideas or data.

The term *personality* is used here to refer to the way a person thinks and behaves in all spheres of life—physical, mental, social, spiritual. It is a term referring to all we are, and so personality study is unbelievably complex. It is quite inaccurate to speak of *personality* as some mystical quality which some people have and others do not have.

Many people have a compulsion to classify personalities according to a system of types. Hippocrates, a Greek physician who lived in the fifth century before Christ, theorized that all persons could be classified according to four types (melancholic, choleric, sanguine, phlegmatic), and these personality types were determined by fluid levels in the body at the time of birth. Others have studied body structure or skull formation as a means of classifying personality. Every psychological system includes a personality theory and for years, Sigmund Freud's ideas on personality have been popular. Also, Carl Jung's distinction between introversion (preoccupied with personal thoughts and feelings) and extroversion (centered on things, facts, activites outside of self) has been used to attempt to classify persons.

The problem with such classification schemes is that the complexity of human personality is obscured by simplistic pigeonholing. Personality is not simple enough to be described in a single type, and where such classification is used, serious distortion often occurs. With regard to career choice, simplistic thinking about personality types usually results in unduly severe limitation of career options. This limitation occurs because the "typing person" does not consider his individual traits, and thus he may overlook important information about himself. Further, this person views careers in a stereotypical manner, assuming that everyone successful in any vocation has the same personality type. Such thinking is both highly inaccurate and quite dangerous.

A more appropriate way of thinking about personality is in terms of personality traits. Traits are groups of related habits in thinking and acting.[5] We may describe ourselves using such traits as reserved, assertive, inhibited, practical, dependent, relaxed, conscientious, and many more. Of course, such traits are still generalizations, but they are more specific than simplistic personality typing and can, therefore, be more helpful to career decisions. Different theorists have estimated that personality traits may number from 170 to about 18,000,[6] and so giving attention to the more predominant ones is usually what occurs in a career decision. Not only do many traits exist, but they exist in degrees. To say that a person is ambitious, for instance, does not say how ambitious he is or whether he is more ambitious than someone else. As we become aware of what traits or characteristics we have, we can inform ourselves regarding which of these would

---

5. Bruce Shertzer, *Career Planning* (Boston: Houghton Mifflin Co., 1977), p. 145.
6. Ibid., p. 146.

likely be fulfilled in various vocations and which might require additional development.

As with any approach, there are dangers in viewing personality solely in terms of traits. One difficulty is semantic confusion, for not everyone means the same thing when speaking of a specific trait. Shyness, for instance, may mean different things in different contexts and to different people. And to say that one is shy does not in itself determine what significance that trait should have in career choice. Another limitation is that defining traits may lead some persons to the conclusion that their personality is static, that they cannot develop or change. This, of course, violates the biblical principle of growth in grace and implies limitation on the edifying grace of God. A third difficulty is that most people are more variable than a strict trait approach would suggest. Children especially are quite inconsistent, and this inconsistency tends to decrease with age. Adolescents, who are making preliminary career choices, may yet be somewhat unsettled in personality traits. It is possible, for instance, to be reserved and sophisticated in some situations, and boisterous and rowdy in others. A fourth limitation is that since so many traits exist, a particular trait may have more relevance to career choice for one person than it would have for another. And the choice of a career may in itself foster the development of certain traits.

With all of these limitations, the examination of personality by looking at various traits can still be effective, because this method seeks to locate each facet of personality and determine its implication for career choice. When we examine our characteristics individually, we face ourselves in a manner that can be productive of growth. We must come to grips with individual traits, examine them, decide whether to strengthen or diminish them, and then use them for God's glory. Such an approach forces us to acknowledge Christ's lordship in all of life.

With a career, one usually chooses a lifestyle. Career is almost always related to lifestyle. This determination relates not only to the amount of money earned, but also to such factors as free time, social status in the community, and the amount of travel in vocation. The lifestyle of an attorney would probably differ from that of a garbage collector, even if they had equivalent salaries, because of the social expectations regarding them. An accountant's lifestyle would differ from a traveling salesman's due, at least, to scheduling and traveling differences. A factory worker, with set hours, would have a different lifestyle than a pastor, who is always on call. These types of considerations need to be faced intelligently, in the light of both commitment and personality, when making a career decision.

It is no doubt true that God occasionally calls some of His children to careers that require drastic adjustment in personality, and these persons may experience hardship in the transition. But such instances serve as special instruction for the Christians involved, and do not necessarily invalidate the general principle. It is interesting to note that the vast majority of prerequisites for the pastorate are *personality traits* that evidence spiritual maturity (I Tim. 3:1-7), not professional competencies.

Personality appraisal is a common practice for everyone; the only difficulty is that we tend to judge everyone else's personality in reference to our own. But self-appraisal is possible and necessary. Personality tests are readily available, but their use needs to be conditioned on an understanding of the test itself, its theoretical base, its strengths and its weaknesses. Examination of our actions can give us insight into our personality dynamics, as can feedback from trusted, insightful friends. Spiritually mature elders in the local church often can discern strengths and weaknesses in the lives of others within their fellowship. The Holy Spirit's testimony, through the Word of God, effectively convicts us of personal shortcomings, which also gives insight into personality.

Desires

A frequent practice among Christians is to speak of sacrificing personal desires in favor of God's will. No doubt many personal desires *should* be sacrificed, since they arise from the world, the flesh, and the devil. Obviously, such desires cannot be followed in a life of godliness, and they would not lead to following the Lord's will.

But does that mean that *every desire* must be discounted or continually suspected? Psalm 37:4 helps answer this question. "Delight yourself in the Lord; and He will give you the desires of your heart." The first part of the verse is crucial. But how do we delight in the Lord? Psalm 37 is a contrast between the evildoer and the righteous person. As an evil person lives for the purpose of evil, and sets all his affections and energies toward evil, so the righteous person is to delight in the Lord, making His righteousness the focus of his living. When we are living with that type of delight in the Lord, He will give us the desires of our hearts. Delighting in the Lord produces such a change in our lives that the desires of our hearts are conformed to His desires for us.

Consequently, we need not always consider our own preferences as opposite to His will for us. God is not a sadistic tyrant who delights in assigning us to life experiences that will antagonize us. When we are living as closely to the Lord as we know how, we can expect Him to give us desires that conform to His desire for us. What a shame it is, after God's work, when

41

we continue to suspect our every desire! Cannot our desires benefit from God's educating grace in sanctification?

When conducting workshops on career choice for Christians, I have often seen students become visibly moved when they grasp this thought. And often, these students ask, "Do you mean that God may really call us to do something we really want to do?" My answer is, "Most definitely!"

Within the career decision, the desires of the faithful believer can be very important. Rather than automatically condemning personal desires, we should examine our living to see whether we are delighting in the Lord. If so, we can use our desires as part of the data necessary for a God-honoring career decision. These desires can prompt investigation into various vocations, and if the vocation is in the Lord's plan, we can expect the desire to increase with increased knowledge and experience.

Unfortunately, some still must speak about "surrendering to the Lord's will" because they have rebelled against it. But such rebellion and eventual surrender is certainly neither the Christian norm nor the preferred practice. The path of blessing is one that consciously seeks an unencumbered fellowship with God, so that desires are not automatically rebellious.

Experiences

Since God is both orderly and personal, the experiences He prepares for us are purposeful. God's intent is to develop us as persons, and consequently, we might expect to learn something from our experiences about His plan for our careers.

How often have we been told to participate in some activity because "It's good experience for you"? We may doubt that the activity itself has much value, but parents and other significant adults seem bent on insuring that we have plenty of "good experiences." Usually, hindsight reveals their wisdom. How do these, and other experiences, help us in making career decisions?

As we evaluate our experiences, we can learn much about ourselves—our interests, abilities, desires, limitations, etc. We can discover our potential for working with others as we survey the experiences that have placed us in contact with other people. Special achievements may give us data about unusual abilities we may possess, as can school or club activities. If experiences include volunteer, part-time, or regular work, these can be especially valuable for learning about work itself and for developing a productive attitude toward its responsibilities.

As we evaluate our experiences, one of the most productive approaches we can take is to look *not* at the experience as a whole, but at specific aspects of it. For instance, it is relatively useless to conclude that a summer job was "a good experience." Rather, we should ask, "What aspects of the job made it a good experience?" Instead of stating that "I liked that course," a more productive approach would be to ask, "What was it about that course that I liked so much?" These preferred questions go beyond generalizations to focus on specific parts of the experiences. As we combine specific aspects from a variety of experiences that appeal to us, we may discern a pattern emerging that can guide us in a career decision.

The following are types of experiences that may profitably be examined to see how God has used them to shape our lives.

Local Church

What activities or ministries in which I have engaged may have implications for career choice?

School Subjects

Which aspects of school courses have excited my interest and abilities? Which have been boring or unreasonably difficult for me? Which involved special projects from which I derived satisfaction?

Employment

What have I learned about myself from part-time, summer, volunteer, or regular jobs? How have different contexts, responsibilities, types of supervision, activities appealed to me?

Hobbies

What specific aspects of my hobbies are of greatest interest that may have vocational implications?

Clubs

What club activities and/or interpersonal relationships may give insight for vocational choice?

Leisure Time Activities

What do I do when I have nothing to do? What interests do these activities reveal?

Careers of Family Members

How have the careers of family members affected me (interest, knowledge, participation, values)?

What experiences have I had that are not available to most persons, and what effects have these experiences had on my development?

Reading

What insights into myself and into various careers have I developed from reading?

There may be other types of experiences that are significant to some people, and these should be studied also. If God truly does lead us on a daily basis (and He does), we should closely scrutinize the things He has done in our lives daily to discern His guidance. God does not reserve His direction until the last moment we can possibly make a decision. Rather, He is continually at work in our lives, even in routine situations, and this activity can give us direction for the future. All of this follows logically from our starting point—God is orderly and personal.

Significant Persons

All of us can name persons who have significant effects on our lives—some for good and some otherwise. Often, persons whom we consider important to us exercise a profound influence on our career choices.

It is not accidental that many enter vocations closely related to their parents' careers. After all, these have had, during their formative years, a first-hand education in the activities, challenges, interests, values, and lifestyles of their parents' careers. The manner in which parents talk about their work in front of their children is bound to affect the children's view of those careers. In fact, one research project among children of missionaries demonstrated that the parents' attitude toward their calling was directly related to their children's plans to be missionaries.[7]

Admiration for parents prompts many children to pattern their lives after their parents', but a rupture of parent-child relations can cause the child to reject much of his parents' lifestyle—and both the admiration and the rupture have a significant effect in career decision. "Following in our parents' footsteps" may be entirely appropriate for some, for parents are usually the primary source of our values which affect career choice. The important factor is not merely whether we are following our parents, or whether parents pressure us to do so, but whether we have examined ourselves adequately so that a choice to enter a parent's vocation is both informed and responsible.

---

7. Theodore Hsieh, "Missionary Family Behavior, Dissonance, and Children's Career Decision," *Journal of Psychology and Theology* 4, no. 3 (Summer 1976): 221-26.

Relatives other than parents frequently affect our career decisions. A respected aunt, uncle, grandparent, or older brother or sister may be engaged in a vocation that has appeal to us. To enter a similar occupation merely out of respect or affection for that relative would be a mistake. But a careful self-study might reveal many similarities with that relative, and so entering a similar vocation might be appropriate.

Other persons significant to us can have the same impact. Affection for a particular teacher has led many to investigate a career in education, and the same could be stated for almost every other vocation imaginable.

Respect or affection for a significant person can be helpful in a career decision, if used correctly. If it is only a blind hero-worship, it may negate proper self-investigation and decision-making. A proper approach would include careful thought on the following questions:

> Why do I have such respect or affection for this person?
> Is my feeling for this person connected in any way with his vocation? or his personality?
> In what ways am I really (or potentially) like this person in abilities, values, and interests?

Christians have yet another advantage in career decisions: godly elders in our churches can give us extremely valuable advice. The Bible abounds with instruction for Christians to minister to one another, and this ministry occurs within the church context (cf. Rom. 15:14; Col. 3:16). The New Testament records the selection of the first missionaries, and it is quite different from the procedure usually used today. Acts 13:1-3 states that the Holy Spirit led the church at Antioch to select Paul and Barnabas to be missionaries and to send them out for ministry. The Spirit's instruction was not only to Paul and Barnabas; it was to the entire church. Godly persons, through prayer, fasting, and ministry, could discern spiritual gifts in others.

In a similar manner, godly persons may help us recognize spiritual gifts and talents in our own lives. We might be suspicious of a church member who says to us, "God told me He wants you to be a beautician"—or missionary, or mechanic, or anything else. Our suspicion arises quite properly, because God has chosen to speak to us through His Word in this age rather than through direct prophecies. But we should take to heart the observation of godly, Bible-taught elders who observe us and recognize our traits. "You have the qualities of a successful mother and homemaker" is the type of insight that should be valued by a young lady facing a career decision. Or, "you can really communicate with children" can be helpful to a young person contemplating a career in education. A person confused

45

about God's plan could benefit from encouragement such as "I've noticed that you have insight into problems, can clarify the real issues, and can make productive decisions." In these instances, the persons receive information about themselves that can be used in a God-honoring career choice.

Likewise, church members have an obligation to admonish one another when they think a fellow-believer is making a mistake. Of course, in doing so, the right attitude is important, for few persons respond well to opinionated or dictatorial advice. But a proper Christian concern should be demonstrated for a believer who may be following an unbiblical value system in a decision, or who may suffer from an inaccurate self-concept.

Often, church members do not offer help in career decisions because they think God's leadership is a mystical force that operates without investigation or information. Others do not get involved for fear their insight will be rejected, or because they do not perceive career choice to be a "spiritual issue" of concern to the church. These misconceptions unfortunately rob many of valuable insight and keep others from the joy of ministering to fellow-believers. It is difficult to imagine anything any "more spiritual" than seeking and doing God's will in life, and helping one another in this process is a fulfilling ministry.

Personal Needs

While many factors are involved in a career decision, the satisfaction of some human need often has significant effect. The term *need* refers to the lack of something required for physical or psychological well-being. Physical needs—survival, safety, monetary income—are very important. If these are not met, life itself does not progress. Few persons select vocations in which their survival or safety is doubtful, especially if there is not a substantial reward for such risk.

Psychological needs may be much more subtle, for they involve such factors as companionship, approval, independence, self-respect, recognition, etc.[8] We must be very cautious, because these *felt* needs may not be *real* needs (i.e., *required* for well-being), but rather, intense desires. In fact, we may try to justify sinful desires by calling them "needs," and our humanistic culture preaches that we *must* have all of these needs met. In fact, in His beatitudes, Christ called on His followers to *seek* several of what the world would call needs. We will use the term "felt needs" to emphasize the distinction between them and real needs. But even with all of these limitations, felt needs are a part of the career choice process.

One who feels a strong need for independence might feel intense frustra-

---

8. Shertzer, op. cit., p. 116.

tion if working in a large organization under close supervision. He would much rather be self-employed and enjoy more independence. One whose felt need for approval iş especially strong may select a vocation that will bring approval of significant persons—parents, spouse, in-laws, church group, or peer group. Self-respect is a powerful force. Many have rejected lucrative but questionable vocational opportunities with the comment, "I just couldn't live with myself if I made a living that way." Such a statement reveals a felt need to accept and like oneself. Recognition, prestige or power can be far more satisfying than money to persons who feel these needs.

Felt needs may have different impact at different times during life. For instance, when a young couple are first married, and a year later have their first baby, the husband may feel a need for high earnings to become financially stable. His job may be in a highly paying trade, and so this need is met. His particular work, however, may offer no opportunity for advancement, and several years later he may switch to a position which offers a lower initial salary but which will challenge him for the future. His felt needs change, and satisfaction requires different career direction.

A college professor's career progress illustrates the force of the felt need for prestige and independence. One's education and experience may qualify him for a high position in industry, but a preference for the prestige and freedom of an academic post leads to a university, even though a teaching salary may be only half what he could earn in industry.

Are different felt needs God-given? To some extent, they probably are. Our perception of our needs is related to our personality, and God develops us with different personalities. Often, though, we think we have needs when in actual fact we are being selfish. Our sinful nature can create a powerful feeling of need. The real issue is not whether we feel needs, but whether these needs are met by biblical means.

Sex-role Concept

What does it mean to be female? to be male?

Our sex is determined at conception, and nothing affects us more physiologically and psychologically than our sex assignment as male or female. And God intended it that way. Scripture records, "God created man in His own image, in the image of God He created him; male and female He created them" (Gen. 1:27). The biblical picture of sex is not so much what we *do* as it is what we *are*. The contemporary distortion and perversion of sexual standards results from viewing sex solely as an activity, whereas the Scripture speaks of it as an integral part of identity.

The roles our culture prescribes for us as male or female often exceed or violate the biblical roles, and they vary from culture to culture, but they are quite potent in their effect on our career decisions. Our American culture has traditionally treated females as passive, emotional, nonintellectual, instinctively maternal, and home-oriented. Males, on the other hand, have been considered to be objective, aggressive, analytical, active, and achievement-oriented. Acceptance of such stereotypes severely limits vocational choices, particularly for the female, but also for the male.

The women's movement is (in part) a response to the frustration experienced by females who refused to be forced into cultural stereotypes. The results have been a gradual dissolution of the stereotypes and a recognition that the traits attributed to women in general were largely fictitious. Consequently, increasing educational and vocational opportunities are being afforded females. The emphasis on women's rights has had a beneficial effect on the Christian community, because it has forced Christian women and men alike to differentiate between biblical roles and cultural expectations.

Another result of the women's movement, however, has been to confuse many regarding the career of homemaking. As more than one bright female student has told me, "I think I would feel guilty if I were to become *only a housewife.*" With many social movements, reaction to correct one extreme often creates another extreme, and that caused the pressure on this student. The career of homemaking was a natural choice for her: it fulfilled her sex-role image, along with her values, interests, creativity, and life-style preferences. A career in homemaking and motherhood will not be the Lord's plan for every female. But by the same token, it is a career to which Scripture ascribes honor, and it is closely related to the meaning of being female for many women. If God's plan for one is to have a homemaking career, it would be a shame if a temporary social movement induced a rebellion against that calling.

Males have not experienced the role confusion vocationally to the extent females have. Our culture has generally rewarded the traits it developed in males. Sex-role concepts do influence decision-making for men as well as for women. One who thinks his masculinity is proved by aggression will probably select a career in which his aggressive desires and actions are rewarded. Many men have no doubt failed to develop talents in the arts or aesthetics because of their mistaken notion that these were more feminine than masculine.

How can we achieve clarity amid cultural confusion regarding sex-roles? The Scripture is clear, and God means for it to guide our values in this as well as other areas of thought and action. Our task is to study the Scripture for an understanding of God's expectations for us and to judge different social philosophies by the standard of His Word.

Conclusion

We have analyzed several factors about ourselves which should be considered in a career decision—abilities, interests, desires, personality traits, experiences, significant others, needs, and sex-role concepts. While the importance attached to each of these factors may vary from person to person, each should be given consideration. In this manner, we honor God by trying to acknowledge all He has placed in our lives. Our investigation does not replace prayer or faith; it is a means of exercising faith.

Perhaps a word or two of caution would be appropriate. First, we should not view ourselves as simply a group of traits measured by tests, or as robots programmed for a single function. Were we able to discover everything possible to know about ourselves (an impossible task), our lives would still amount to more than the sum of these traits.

Second, while we may have some traits that are very similar to those of others, we must remember that we are unique persons. Attempting to pattern our lives after someone else is an exercise of self-deception that results in frustration and guilt. Acceptance and appreciation of ourselves as unique creations of the God of all grace normally leads to a more profound consecration of all of life to Him.

Finally, we should not think of self-appraisal as an event occurring only once in life, but as a continuing process. Personality, experiences, interests, abilities, desires, needs—they all change over a period time. Sometimes change occurs by our deliberate effort, but usually it happens gradually and without our conscious intent. Change should be expected, since Scripture encourages us to grow (cf. II Pet. 1:5-8; Heb. 5:11-14). But growth brings with it the challenge of increased responsibility to know ourselves so we can intelligently and faithfully serve Christ with all we are and all we have.

ACTIVITIES FOR PERSONAL INVENTORY

1. List the three things you like most about yourself.

   1.

   2.

   3.

2. If you could change anything about yourself, what three things would you change?

   1.

   2.

   3.

3. Interview two adult leaders in your church, asking them what personality traits and aptitudes they have noticed in you that would be helpful to you in your career decision. Record their responses.

Name: _____   Response: _____

_____

_____

_____

_____

Name: _____   Response: _____

_____

_____

_____

_____

4. If you are in school, talk to your guidance counselor about taking a vocational interest test. If you take such a test, list below the top five interests your test results indicated. Then ask yourself, "What specific activities within each vocation interest me the most?"

	Vocations	Most interesting activities
1.	_____	_____
		_____
2.	_____	_____
		_____
3.	_____	_____
		_____
4.	_____	_____
		_____
5.	_____	_____
		_____

Remember the limitations of tests. They may provide some helpful data for your decisions, but they cannot tell you what you *should* do.

5. Have you had any experiences (travel, hobbies, achievements, etc.) which most people do not have? If so, how can these experiences influence your career alternatives?

6. Have you made career choices before, but later changed your mind? Specifically, what prompted you to change your mind? What can you learn from the experience that will help you in future career decisions?

7. What do your experiences tell you about your *abilities?* In the following experience categories, list the school subjects, hobbies, church activities, etc. in which you have successfully participated. Then list the specific factors of each activity which made it interesting, and the abilities you used in these activities, and also any limitations you discovered you have.

Experiences	Abilities Demonstrated	Limitations Demonstrated
(1) School Subjects		
_____	_____	_____
_____	_____	_____
_____	_____	_____
_____	_____	_____
_____	_____	_____
_____	_____	_____
_____	_____	_____

(2) Church Activities

_____   _____   _____

_____   _____   _____

_____   _____   _____

_____   _____   _____

_____   _____   _____

_____   _____   _____

(3) Extracurricular Activities, Clubs, Sports, etc.

_____   _____   _____

_____   _____   _____

_____   _____   _____

_____   _____   _____

(4) Work Experiences

_____   _____   _____

_____   _____   _____

_____   _____   _____

_____   _____   _____

_____   _____   _____

(5) Hobbies

_____   _____   _____

_____   _____   _____

_____   _____   _____

_____   _____   _____

_____   _____   _____

(6) Other Experiences

_____   _____   _____

_____   _____   _____

_____   _____   _____

_____   _____   _____

_____   _____   _____

8. What do your experiences tell you about your *interests?* In each of the
   following categories, list the school subjects, hobbies, church activities,
   etc. in which you have successfully participated. Then list the specific
   factors of each activity which made it interesting, and the specific factors
   which were not interesting.

Experiences   Interests   Non-Interests

(1) School Subjects

_____   _____   _____

_____   _____   _____

_____   _____   _____

_____ _____ _____

_____ _____ _____

(2) Church Activities

_____ _____ _____

_____ _____ _____

_____ _____ _____

_____ _____ _____

_____ _____ _____

(3) Extracurricilar Activities, Clubs, Sports, etc.

_____ _____ _____

_____ _____ _____

_____ _____ _____

_____ _____ _____

_____ _____ _____

(4) Work Experiences

_____ _____ _____

_____ _____ _____

_____ _____ _____

_____ _____ _____

(5) Hobbies

_____   _____   _____

_____   _____   _____

_____   _____   _____

_____   _____   _____

_____   _____   _____

(6) Other Experiences

_____   _____   _____

_____   _____   _____

_____   _____   _____

_____   _____   _____

_____   _____   _____

5 *Decision Making*

Many believers suspect that a thoughtful, logical decision-making process excludes God's leadership. Obviously, we sometimes *do* make decisions without spiritual insight, but those failures should not lead us to abandon the search for a proper, spiritual approach to decisions.

Decision making does not occur in a vacuum. When we make decisions, we reflect our values, our view of ourselves and of our environment, our backgrounds, our faith, our personality traits, and numerous other factors. Rather than ignoring all of this and seeking a mystical experience to label "God's leading," we need to acknowledge that God is Lord over every aspect of life. He therefore is at work in all the factors involved in any decision. This broad view of the sovereignty of God is the basis for the decision-making model that follows. The approach is to implement what we know about God in a decision model, rather than to attempt to support every point of the model with a specific Bible verse.

Crucial to any decision is the person making it. Consequently, we will focus first on "the decider," and then on the decision-making process itself.

The Decider

How we see ourselves (self-concept) affects several dimensions of our decision making. For instance, some persons see themselves as "take charge deciders" who see a need for making a decision and who become impatient if forced to remain in ambiguity. Others, however, see themselves above problems (or, perhaps, below them), and see no need for decisions (or no ability to decide correctly). Some are active in attacking a problem, and others remain passive, assuming any problem will eventually resolve itself. Some assume all problems are solvable, while others seem overwhelmed when faced with choices. Some are never satisfied, others are satisfied with only the optimum outcome, and still others will be satisfied with practically anything. Some can tolerate great risk and will make career choices that are quite daring, and others value security and grasp choices already within their reach.

Our perceptual set (what we recognize on a conscious level) is also important, because it determines what we will perceive to be viable alternatives for our decisions. We simply will not choose an alternative that has never occurred to us. The more we know, the better our decisions will be. Perception is greatly restricted by prejudice, by blindly accepting culturally imposed stereotypes. God offers "peace that passes understanding," but He nowhere promises peace that flourishes in place of knowledge or understanding. Our perceptual range is broadened and rendered more accurate by increasing knowledge.

Most important is the decider's value system. A value is simply a determination of the worth of something (an idea, a person, an object, etc.). We express a value when we say something is "good," or that it is "better" than something else. Some things are good because of their intrinsic worth, others because they function well as instruments of achieving something else that has worth. We are never without values; in fact every choice reflects some value (or values). For instance, choosing to deposit money into a savings account rather than to spend it for an evening of entertainment reflects the comparative values one attaches to money, to savings (security), and to entertainment. Choosing to read this book rather than one on some other topic probably reflects some value you attach to this subject matter, considering it of more value to you at this time than the value of some other topic.

The problem we most frequently face with values is that we usually expect them to operate intuitively, outside our conscious thought and control. This approach must be challenged by the Christian; for him, values must be held at the conscious level so that his belief structure may be involved in the decision. It is in the area of values that the Scripture gives specific guidance. Often admonished to read the Bible to find direction, we may frequently feel frustrated because we cannot find a particular verse that speaks directly to our questions. We may then conclude that the Scripture is deficient, or we may resort to some artificial "flip-plop" method ("flip" open the Bible, "plop" down a finger on a verse at random), and expect an answer from it.

A consistent, systematic study of the Bible, however, ought to result in the formation of biblical values. The degree of understanding of the Scripture, and commitment to it, usually corresponds to the degree of scriptural influence on one's value structure. Values, then, are reflections of our beliefs. A faithful study of God's Word may *not* give a specific verse upon which we might hang a career choice, but it will affect the values underlying that choice. It will shape the "decider."

58

Specific values to which the Scripture speaks may include the following:

Nature of life (time)
>work
>money and lifestyle
>stewardship concepts
>achievement
>success
>life goals
>security
>witness
>family
>service

These all have bearing on career decisions, and the Bible guides our decisions to the extent that its teachings are consciously sought and followed in these value areas.

The Decision-Making Process

1. *Recognizing a decision must be made*

Some follow the theory that no decision is necessary, that all planning is irrelevant, because they think that only one alternative will be available to them at any one time. Since God's program involves human responsibility, that approach seldom will produce a God-honoring result. It places one at the mercy of circumstances, not under the operation of faith. Decisions and planning are necessary to the proper exercise of obedient faith.

2. *Defining the problem/decision*

What is involved in the decision, and what is not involved? While a career decision may have a relationship to other decisions (e.g., marriage, purchase of a new car, etc.), it may not involve these other factors directly.

Usually, career choices are made with some precedents. Deciding to enroll in a college course, for instance, may lead to a later career choice, but a clear understanding of an eventual career is usually not necessary for one to enroll in a course. In fact, experimenting in "minor" decisions can greatly enhance ability in making "major" ones.

Enrolling in a college course, for instance, might generate in a student sufficient interest for him or her to take more courses in the same area (course concentration), or it might not. Similarly, a concentration may or may not lead to a college major. And graduation with a specific major does not automatically assure the student will select a job directly related to his major. Further, the first job does not determine the course of an entire career.

Changes are frequently made in each of these stages, as illustrated below.

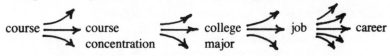

If we do not take time to define a problem, we may enlarge it completely out of proportion to reality. This only intensifies the difficulty of early decision making and frustrates the entire process.

3. *Informing self*

As noted earlier, a problem afflicting many Christians is an erroneous notion that the Holy Spirit's leadership makes information and research unnecessary. Faithful decision making, however, attempts to account for what God has already done and how He has already led in our lives. Consequently, we need to inform ourselves about ourselves and about our opportunities.

The factors we should consider about ourselves have been discussed in chapter 4. Reviewing briefly, we should examine the following:

abilities and limitations
interests
personality traits
desires
experiences
significant persons
personal needs
sex-role concepts

Various methods for investigating each of these were noted also in chapter 4.

Gathering information on opportunities usually involves investigation of a vocation's usual characteristics. Factors for consideration may include the following:

activities performed in the vocation (people/things/ideas/data)
responsibilities to the employer
abilities, education, and experience required
probable salary range; other benefits
available and potential openings
time demands
opportunities for advancement
values expressed in the work
accompanying lifestyle
types of pressure involved
effect of automation, both present and future
effect of inflation and/or recession on the vocation

nature of job security or risk
compatibility of the total job with Christian beliefs
relationships to other vocations
necessity of frequent relocation
nature of Christian witness opportunities

Many other factors may be considered, depending upon the vocations in question. Firm determination regarding God's leading does not usually come from superficial understanding, but rather accompanies thorough investigation. Christ considered persons to be wise who first counted the cost before undertaking a task (Luke 14:28-32). The life of faith is lived by informed commitment, not ignorant stubbornness.

How, then, can we learn all we need to know in order to make a good decision? Every decision involves some risk, but this risk can be minimized greatly if we take the time to examine the information available. Following are common sources of career information.

a. *Occupational Outlook Handbook*

Published every other year by the U.S. Department of Labor, this book includes job descriptions, requirements, opportunities, and sources of more information on approximately 800 occupations. It can usually be found in any public or school library, as well as in virtually all school guidance offices and college counseling centers.

b. *Dictionary of Occupational Titles*

Published by the U.S. Department of Labor, this volume gives brief descriptions of over 30,000 occupations.

c. *Professional associations*

Hundreds of professional associations (e.g., American Medical Association, etc.) exist, and most of these publish brochures describing their profession, and they distribute the literature at no charge.

d. *Periodical articles*

Magazines such as *Business Week* and *U.S. News and World Report* (and many others) often include informative articles on specific careers. The *Readers Guide to Periodic Literature* (in all libraries) can help you locate such articles on careers that interest you.

e. *Books*

Entire books on specific careers are usually available in public and school libraries.

f. *Guidance offices, counseling centers*

These offices normally include extensive career files with current information on numerous careers.

g. *Career days*

Special "career days" or "career fairs" are often sponsored by schools, colleges, or by local chambers of commerce. These events afford good opportunity to talk to knowledgeable persons and collect information on a variety of vocations from numerous companies.

h. *Interviews*

Interviewing persons actively engaged in a vocation can give interesting, personal insight into that particular calling and can be a helpful method of getting pressing questions answered.

i. *Newspapers*

Some newspapers print regular columns on careers which can be informative. The classified advertisements of large city newspapers can include a wealth of information on job opportunities, requirements, salaries, companies, etc.

j. *Placement Agencies*

State employment offices, commercial employment services, or school and college placement agencies can often supply information on employment trends as well as on specific vocations.

The more we know about a vocation, the better we can judge how our abilities, interests, and values fit that particular calling. Also, such investigation might prompt us to look for previously undetected talents, develop latent abilities, or reexamine our interests or values. The purpose of all this information is not to by-pass faith or to minimize trust in God's leading, but to demonstrate a responsible faith by utilizing material God has already provided. Consequently, the thorough study of vocational options is not an escape from trust, from prayer, or from a sense of calling. It is, rather, a responsible effort to be a good steward of life. Ignorance is no friend of faith.

4. *Generating creative alternatives*

The data we accumulate about ourselves and our opportunities should suggest a number of vocational alternatives. We can generate even more alternatives by isolating each piece of data we have about ourselves and trying to imagine as many jobs as we can that would utilize that particular interest, ability, value, etc. This is not the point for emphasizing hindrances, realistic or otherwise. The main responsibility at this stage is to think of as many alternatives as possible.

A problem frequently occurs if we look for the feeling of peace in our decision process. Seeking a feeling of peace as an indication of God's approval often leads us to inferior decisions by cutting the process short at this stage. If we face a decision in which we think there is *no* answer, or in which we think the answer will come with great difficulty, then we will feel great relief when we discover one possible solution. This relief is then construed as the "peace of God," and no more alternatives are sought. It is questionable whether such relief really does signify God's leadership, since it is an emotional reaction experienced by believers and unbelievers alike.

By generating a number of alternatives, however, we run less chance of limiting God in leading us. Also, we are more likely to utilize a variety of the traits God has given us. Creative alternatives will focus on implementing these traits without stereotyped thinking about specific careers.

As a list of alternatives grows, its value increases. The real value lies not so much in the alternatives themselves as in our use of them. A productive use of alternatives involves examining each to see what factor or factors are appealing to us. For instance, an alternative of "computer programmer" may be helpful, even if one does not become a programmer, because he might determine that certain facets of that vocation appeal to him (e.g., work with data, problem solving, limited people contact, etc.). By examining numerous alternatives in this way, certain factors may emerge repeatedly, and these may be combined creatively into a suitable alternative. The wise decision maker will probably distill various appealing traits from his list of alternatives and then ask himself: "How can I combine these traits into the ideal vocation for me?" Each new alternative formed then requires us to gather some information before we can proceed to the next step.

5. *Evaluating alternatives*

After a list of alternatives is formed (and, of course, written), each entry should be evaluated. Some might be completely unrealistic and eliminated fairly quickly. Even these, however, can be helpful in highlighting certain appealing factors (as discussed in the previous step).

The alternatives that remain (along with their anticipated outcomes) should be evaluated in the light of a personal value system. Those alternatives formed by combining traits in the previous step should receive special attention, since they will probably conform to personal values more closely than the others.

Values deal with the desirability of something. Consequently, they are directly affected by an understanding of ourselves and of the Word of God. When we evaluate (or "set a value upon") our opportunities, we are determining their relative importance to us. Often, our question is not so much one of "value versus no value," but one of varying degrees of value. (Later exercises are designed to clarify the relationship of values.)

Following is a list of values that usually apply to career decisions.[1] While additional values sometimes may be operating, and some of the following occasionally may be irrelevant, the list can provide a beginning for examining our values. Several values were listed earlier in this chapter (under "The Decider") to which the Scripture probably speaks more directly, and they are not repeated here.

Help Society: do something to contribute to the betterment of the world in general.

Help Other People: be involved in helping specific people directly.

People Contact: have much daily contact with different people.

Cooperation: work with others as a team toward common goals.

Affiliation: receive recognition as a member of a particular group.

Friendships: develop close personal relationships with people as a part of the working activities.

Competition: motivate self by comparing abilities with others in clearly defined win/lose situations.

Pressure: work in situations in which time pressure is prevalent and/or the quality of work is judged critically by supervisors, customers, or others.

Decision Making: have power to decide policies, procedures, etc.

Authority: control and evaluate the work of others.

Influence: change the attitudes or opinions of other people.

Investigation: engage in research, the pursuit of knowledge.

Intellectual status: attain recognition as intellectual or expert.

Creativity: create something not previously developed by others (e.g., art forms, organizations, programs, ideas, solutions, etc.).

Aesthetics: study or appreciate the beauty of things.

Supervision: be responsible for work done by others.

Variety: have responsibilities that frequently change in their content and/or setting..

1. Adapted from Howard E. Figler, *PATH: A Career Workbook for Liberal Arts Students* (Cranston, R. I.: Carroll Press, 1975), pp. 77-79.

Stability: have duties that are routine, predictable, and not likely to change over a period of time.

Security: have assurance of keeping the job with reasonable financial reward.

Activity level: work in circumstances in which there is a fast pace of activity.

Recognition: receive recognition in a visible or public way for the quality of work.

Excitement: experience a high degree of or frequent excitement in the course of the work.

Adventure: have responsibilities involving frequent risk.

Money: have a strong prospect for accumulating material gain.

Independence: work alone, without significant contact with other people.

Autonomy: be able to determine the nature and functions of work without significant direction from others (do as one pleases).

Closure: be able to see specific results of work regularly.

Location: live in a place conducive to preferred lifestyle (availability of specific activities, church, community involvement, etc.).

Physical Challenge: be rewarded by meeting physical demands.

Time Freedom: be able to work according to one's own schedule and deadlines (when one pleases).

Spiritual Fulfillment: understanding that the work is contributing significantly to spiritual standards that are considered important.

Many students have never thought seriously about such values, and so their focus needs to be on the values themselves before evaluating alternatives using the values. Some have made good career decisions without going through such a process, but their experiences should not establish the norm for others. Rather, judging our alternatives by our values best utilizes all we know about ourselves and all we believe from our study of God's Word.

Since working with a number of alternatives can become confusing, it is always a good idea to write out the various alternatives and the values operating in each. Not only does writing increase objectivity, it assures that each value will receive appropriate attention. If we take several weeks (or months) with a particular career choice, we will think of numerous alternatives and various reasons why each of these might be accepted or rejected. Committing all of this to writing is important; otherwise all of the effort may be wasted. Without a record of these thoughts, the decision may be based only on how we feel on the decision day, or only on the most recent alternative to occur to us.

6. *Choosing among alternatives*

No amount of preparation will totally eliminate all risk from a career decision. We cannot know the future, and we are fallible in our understanding of our past and present. Consequently, this decision-making plan will not rid us of mistakes. But it will minimize mistakes by promoting faithfulness in accounting for much of what God has already done for us.

The actual choice of a career objective could be made in several stages. The list of alternatives could be narrowed to perhaps three or four by means of tentative choices (plural). These choices are not final, but narrowing allows more intensive research and prayer regarding them. Perhaps this research and prayer will prepare for the next step—a tentative choice (singular). Further research may involve taking some courses in the area chosen, or securing a part-time job closely connected to the choice. The tentative choices are intended as opportunities for in-depth exploration. In these stages, we are looking for confirmation (assurance) that our choices fit the abilities, interests, values, etc., that God has placed in our lives.

Then, the decision is actually made. The experiences from our research and prayer frequently lead us to reaffirm our tentative choice. If that does not occur, we should give particular attention to other tentative choices. If these do not meet our criteria either, we should revert to stages 3 or 4 and begin the process again at that point.

7. *Evaluation*

Once a decision is made, continual evaluation is needed. Perhaps later school or work experiences are not what we anticipated, and it might be that we have made a mistake. There is certainly no disgrace in making an appropriate change, but remaining in poorly chosen jobs can produce frustration.

Continual evaluation is also necessary when we are enjoying our work. Certain abilities may become obsolete (perhaps due to automation), and we may be forced to change careers even though we may have been happy and successful. New abilities likewise may be acquired, opening new alternatives that deserve consideration. Interests may change, and so might work values, lifestyle preferences, health, and many other factors.

A career is normally more than a single job. Usually, a career is a succession of jobs throughout one's work life. Making changes, then, is often not a symptom of a problem but rather a consequence of success. Mid-career changes may involve moving "up the ladder," or they might involve significant changes in direction. At each of these points, evaluation becomes necessary. Making significant changes without thoroughly "counting the cost'' does not please God and does not result in satisfaction for us. The evaluation will probably follow the evaluation plan outlined above in step 5.

Should the Lord lead (through the evaluation) to change from the present status, the decision-making process begins all over again. If a change is not indicated, then continuation should be assumed.

The obvious implication from this evaluation process is that career decision making should occur throughout one's career. Too often, the career decision is viewed as a once-in-a-lifetime event, made during or shortly after high school. This view causes frustration in those who later face decisions. They think they should have to make only the single choice, and everything will quite naturally fall into place after that. Not only does this once-in-a-lifetime view contradict the realities of our present world, it also fails to promote an attitude of thoughtful stewardship of all of life.

Summary

The following diagram summarizes the decision-making process as described in this chapter. When reducing a complicated, multi-faceted process like decision making to a diagram, the charge of being overly simplistic might be appropriate. The diagram, however, can visually clarify important steps we may be overlooking. Also it can challenge us to be orderly in our choices, conscious that our choices affect our lives significantly.

Career Decision-making Model

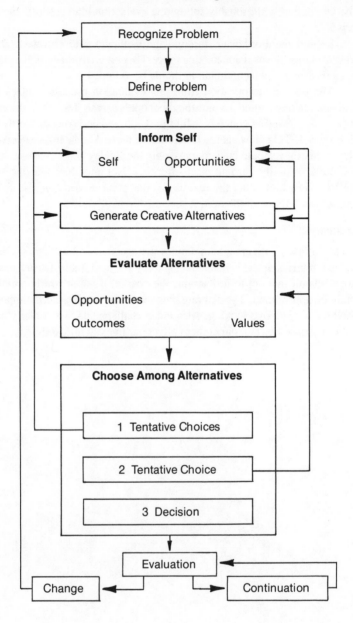

ACTIVITIES FOR PERSONAL INVENTORY[2]

1. Circle the number that describes the importance you attach to each of the following values (1 = little importance; 5 = great importance).

1 2 3 4 5   Help society: do something to contribute to the betterment of the world in general.

1 2 3 4 5   Help other people: be involved in helping specific people directly.

1 2 3 4 5   People contact: have much daily contact with different people.

1 2 3 4 5   Cooperation: work with others as a team toward common goals.

1 2 3 4 5   Affiliation: receive recognition as a member of a particular group.

1 2 3 4 5   Friendships: develop close personal relationships with people as a part of the working activities.

1 2 3 4 5   Competition: motivate self by comparing abilities with others in clearly defined win/lose situations.

1 2 3 4 5   Pressure: work in situations in which time pressure is prevalent and/or the quality of work is judged critically by supervisors, customers, or others.

1 2 3 4 5   Decision making: have power to decide policies, procedures, etc.

1 2 3 4 5   Authority: control and evaluate the work of others.

1 2 3 4 5   Influence: change the attitudes or opinions of other people.

---

2. Adapted from ibid.

1 2 3 4 5   Investigation: engage in research, the pursuit of knowledge.

1 2 3 4 5   Intellectual status: attain recognition as intellectual or expert.

1 2 3 4 5   Creativity: create something not previously developed by others (e.g., art forms, organizations, programs, ideas, solutions, etc.).

1 2 3 4 5   Aesthetics: study or appreciate the beauty of things.

1 2 3 4 5   Supervision: be responsible for work done by others.

1 2 3 4 5   Variety: have responsibilities that frequently change in their content and/or setting.

1 2 3 4 5   Stability: have duties that are routine, predictable, and not likely to change over a period of time.

1 2 3 4 5   Security: have assurance of keeping the job with reasonable financial reward.

1 2 3 4 5   Activity level: work in circumstances in which there is a fast pace of activity.

1 2 3 4 5   Recognition: receive recognition in a visible or public way for the quality of work done.

1 2 3 4 5   Excitement: experience a high degree of or frequent excitement in the course of work.

1 2 3 4 5   Adventure: have responsibilities involving frequent risk.

1 2 3 4 5   Money: have a strong prospect for accumulating material gain.

1 2 3 4 5   Independence: work alone, without significant contact with other people.

1 2 3 4 5　　　　Autonomy: be able to determine the nature and functions of work without significant direction from others (do as one pleases).

1 2 3 4 5　　　　Closure: be able to see specific results of work regularly.

1 2 3 4 5　　　　Location: live in a place conducive to preferred lifestyle (availability of specific activities, church, community involvement, etc.).

1 2 3 4 5　　　　Physical challenge: be rewarded by meeting physical demands.

1 2 3 4 5　　　　Time freedom: be able to work according to one's own schedule and deadlines (when one pleases).

1 2 3 4 5　　　　Spiritual fulfillment: understanding that the work is contributing significantly to spiritual standards that are considered important.

2. From the preceding list, select the four values of most importance to you, and then list three careers in which these values would operate.

Value 1 _____   _____

_____

_____

Value 2 _____   _____

_____

_____

Value 3 _____   _____

                                    _____

                                    _____

Value 4 _____   _____

                                    _____

                                    _____

3. Select three vocations in which you are presently interested and then find four sources of current information describing them.

Sources Consulted

Vocation   1:   _____   _____   _____

                                 _____   _____

Vocation   2:   _____   _____   _____

                                 _____   _____

Vocation   3:   _____   _____   _____

                                 _____   _____

4. List three decisions you have recently made in any area of your life. Then, reflect on how you made each decision. Did you gather information, generate alternatives, evaluate alternatives by your values, pray? Then suggest any way you could have improved the process of each of these decisions.

Decision 1 _____

Information Gathered	_Alternatives_	_Important Values_
_____	_____	_____
_____	_____	_____
_____	_____	_____
_____	_____	_____

Prayer involvement: yes _____ no _____

Suggested improvements:

Decision 2 _____

Information Gathered	_Alternatives_	_Important Values_
_____	_____	_____
_____	_____	_____
_____	_____	_____
_____	_____	_____

Prayer involvement: yes _____ no _____

Suggested improvements:

Decision 3 _____

Information Gathered	*Alternatives*	*Important Values*
_____	_____	_____
_____	_____	_____
_____	_____	_____
_____	_____	_____

Prayer involvement: yes _____ no _____

Suggested improvements:

6 *Spiritual Gifts and Career Choice*

Spiritual gifts are the exclusive possession of those in whom the Holy Spirit dwells, and the Holy Spirit is in the life of every Christian (Romans 8:9). Even though these gifts are essential to the dynamic functioning of Christ's church, many Christians are confused about them. Some consider these gifts to be the privilege of a small group, a spiritual elite, who exercise them in a spectacular manner. Others, noting flagrant abuse of spiritual gifts, withdraw even from discussing them. Not only do spiritual gifts provide immeasureable blessing to Christians who understand them, they also can provide a valuable source of guidance in the career decision.

The topic of spiritual gifts could be dealt with appropriately in chapter 3 ("The Person God Has Made"), for these gifts are certainly part of God's work in forming our lives. But to emphasize this work of God and its potential impact on career choice, I have devoted a separate chapter to this subject.

What Are Spiritual Gifts?

A spiritual gift is simply "a God-given ability for service."[1] The New Testament word usually translated "gifts" emphasizes that they are the result of God's grace, therefore given to believers by God at His own initiative and apart from human merit. The three Scripture passages which contain the bulk of the teaching on spiritual gifts (Rom. 12; I Cor. 12-14, Eph. 4) speak of them as operating within the church, the body of Christ. While *every believer* has at least one spiritual gift, no one is authorized to use his gift solely for his own benefit, "for to each one is given the manifestation of the Spirit for the common good" (I Cor. 12:7).

Since a spiritual gift is primarily an ability, it should not be confused with an office, or a sphere in which the ability is exercised. Since the New Testament church had only two permanent offices, pastor (elder, bishop) and deacon, and since these were likely held by men only, it is obvious that the remainder of the Christians in each congregation exercised their gifts apart from specific offices or positions within the church.

---

1. Charles C. Ryrie, *Balancing the Christian Life* (Chicago: Moody Press, 1969), p. 94.

What Are the Spiritual Gifts?

The three New Testament passages listing spiritual gifts do not include exactly the same gifts, but the following classification is made by combining these lists. Scripture does *not* teach that all the gifts are to operate throughout the church age, but it does imply that gifts especially suited for the initiation of the Christian age would cease operation as the gospel era progressed (I Cor. 13:8-10).

Certain gifts were given for and uniquely suited to the age prior to the completion of the New Testament. Prophecy, for instance, included communicating God's revelation, and the gift of discerning spirits functioned to discern between true and false prophets. With the closing of the New Testament canon, such communicative functions ceased (I Cor. 13:8; Rev. 22:18). Likewise, the apostleship was a gift bestowed on 15 persons (the twelve, Paul, James, Barnabas) enabling these individuals to function authoritatively in the formation of the church (Eph. 2:20). There is no evidence in Scripture that the apostleship was transmitted or otherwise given to anyone else. As the apostles discharged their God-given functions, gifts of miracles (including healing) were entrusted to them to serve as God's authentication of His message (II Cor. 12:12; Rom. 15:18-19). In a similar manner, the gifts of speaking in an unlearned language and the resulting interpretation (translation) were given as signs, probably to unbelieving Jews (I Cor. 14:20-22). The gift of knowledge was especially important prior to the completion of Scripture, since it provided special insight or intuition beyond the normal (I Cor. 12:8; 13:8). The special gifts of wisdom and knowledge (I Cor. 12:8) were temporary, and they probably involved receiving special revelation in doctrinal and practical matters respectively.[2]

Other gifts coincide with scriptural admonitions that apply to all Christians. Helping, showing mercy, and giving are called spiritual gifts (Rom. 12:7-8). While some have more opportunity than others for efforts in these areas, each of these gifts is appropriate to every believer.[3] Similarly, all are challenged to have a strong faith (Matt. 17:20; 21:21). The gift of faith probably refers not to saving faith, but to a wonder-working faith.[4] While these illustrations show that all believers can possess and exercise several spiritual gifts, they also show that the believer has a responsibility for the development of his gifts.

---

2. Robert G. Gromacki, *Called to Be Saints* (Grand Rapids: Baker Book House, 1977) p. 153.

3. Ryrie, pp. 96-97.

4. A. T. Robinson, *Word Pictures in the New Testament* (Nashville: Broadman Publishing Co., 1943), 4:169.

The gift of helps probably refers to a special concern for and ministry to the needy (I Cor. 12:28). While something all believers should demonstrate (James 1:27), special abilities in handling troubled people may be indicated by this gift. This same ability is elsewhere called the gift of ministering or serving (Rom. 12:7). Likewise, all believers are to be sound-minded, but the gift of governments (or rule, or administration) probably implies a special ability to exercise sound judgment (I Cor. 12:28; Rom. 12:8). The gift of exhortation probably involves encouragement or persuasiveness in helping others grow in the faith (Rom. 12:8), and some believers seem particularly gifted for this function.

Three gifts appear to be more closely related to specific offices than the others. The gift of pastor (Eph. 4:11) enables one to protect and to nurture the people of God, the word itself picturing this protection as that which a shepherd exercises toward his sheep. Though this is obviously the function of one in the office of pastor, individuals other than those holding pastoral offices are able to protect and edify their fellow believers. If gifts are seen as abilities, then it is quite reasonable to expect the abilities to appear in individuals other than officeholders.

Evangelism is listed as a gift (Eph. 4:11), and it probably refers to the ability to announce the gospel effectively to those who have not previously heard it. While every Christian has the responsibility and privilege of witnessing, the gift of evangelism evidently implies a special ability to communicate truth (perhaps stating profound biblical concepts in a simple, easily understood manner).

The gift of teaching involves the ability to prompt the learning of God's revelation (I Cor. 12:28; Rom. 12:7; Eph. 4:11). The teacher does not receive revelation from God (as did apostles and prophets), but is able to organize and explain the revelation already received. Teaching is a part of the pastor's role, but is listed apart from the pastorate in I Corinthians 12:28, thereby indicating that others also possess and exercise this gift (cf. Titus 2:3; Heb. 5:12).

Spiritual gifts are given by God to believers as He chooses, and this gifting process is likened to a physical body to show that every believer has some gift (I Cor. 12:11-18). Rather than assuming that spiritual gifts are only for the exceptional saints, all of us have the responsibility of discovering and exercising our gifts.

Discovering Your Spiritual Gifts

Charles C. Ryrie has given three excellent suggestions for discovering spiritual gifts.[5] First, we must *be informed,* for misinformation can rob us of significant blessing. Not knowing the role or nature of the gifts can effectively cripple Christian living. Second, we must *be willing* to be used by the Lord as He directs, perhaps exercising our gifts in a variety of contexts. Perhaps a thoughtful sacrifice or a reordering of life's priorities will be necessary to submit to the lordship of the Spirit, who distributes gifts according to His will. Third, we must *be active.* Given the list of gifts, everyone has some place to start (such as in showing mercy or in giving). Faithfully using such a gift will likely lead to the discovery of some other gift.

Career Insight from Spiritual Gifts

As one discovers, develops, and exercises his spiritual gifts in the local assembly of believers, he will gain insight into himself as a unique creation of God. This insight, then, can lead to informed, Spirit-led decisions about career direction.

A Christian, for instance, who serves other members of Christ's family by teaching in Sunday school, Bible clubs, small groups, etc., may discover that he has the gift of teaching. In this case, faithfulness to the Lord in the use of a gift for the benefit of others would lead to greater self-understanding. Normally, this gift would involve a readiness in understanding a subject area and an ability in communicating it effectively. As an individual observes how the students learn, how he enjoys the process of teaching, and how he is evaluated, he can come to some conclusion regarding his gift of teaching. He could be equally helped if the students do not learn, if he does not enjoy the process, or if he is given a poor evaluation. He might learn from this experience that he should not pursue teaching. Because one has the gift of teaching and exercises it effectively within the church does not necessarily mean that his career should be in education. But at the same time, he should consider it among his career options.

Similarly, a young person may demonstrate leadership potential in a church youth group. Perhaps he is able to conduct business meetings, to organize outings, and to delegate responsibilities to others in the group effectively. These emerging abilities are quite probably indicators that the young person has the spiritual gift of administration. While the gift enables him to serve his fellow-believers in the church, it also gives him insight into the person God has made him. Abilities in organizing, planning, challenging, overseeing and evaluating are all involved in the life of one with this gift. Among the various possibilities he examines for his career should

---

5. Ryrie, pp. 99-101.

be those utilizing the management abilities he has already demonstrated through his gift.

As another example, a Christian may have the gift of ministry (or helps), and that may be evidenced by activity that genuinely helps others. Perhaps others seek him out for advice in problems, for direction in their lives, or for relief in some type of difficulty. The one who ministers does so by helping bear some burden, normally being prompted by a feeling of genuine love. Since burdens may involve nearly every facet of life, helps should be viewed as a very broad gift encompassing a wide variety of activities. Helping one person may involve listening and advising, while helping another might necessitate fixing plumbing, setting up a budget, or showing hospitality to a guest. Whatever other abilities are utilized, this gift probably is marked by an activity orientation (one who actually *does* something of practical help, rather than plan or talk about it). If the helping person sees himself being effectively used by God in this manner, and if he finds the helping experiences particularly satisfying, he would be wise to investigate careers in which these same abilities could be utilized. Many social service careers, for instance, would require similar abilities and personality traits.

The spiritual gift of exhortation involves encouragement or persuasion, normally toward the goal of spiritual growth. While acknowledging this gift does not operate without the concurrent persuasion by the Holy Spirit, it may involve abilities that have career implications. Exhortation is a people-oriented gift in which the aim is not so much to communicate information as it is to persuade people to act on the information. Kenneth Gangel has made the interesting observation that perhaps church musicians may be exercising this gift because of the persuasive and encouraging functions of music (there is no specific "gift of music" mentioned in the New Testament).[6] Many careers involve persuasion, such as counseling, sales, management, communications, numerous Christian service vocations, etc. While not equating the gift of exhortation with the ability to persuade on any topic, persuasion is a part of the gift and it might have career applications beyond its use within the church.

Showing mercy is the gift which operates when one Christian sympathizes with another who is ill or afflicted in some way. Some people cannot stand being around illness or suffering, but the believer gifted in mercy feels comfortable when helping these needy persons. This gift may not correspond exactly to specific careers outside the church, but it might give career direction to those possessing it. One who can show mercy might profit

---

6. Kenneth O. Gangel, *You and Your Spiritual Gifts* (Chicago: Moody Press, 1975), p. 30.

from investigating the careers in which he could work directly with ill persons or other needy people. Various health sciences and human or social services, for instance, might be appropriate for inquiry.

The gift of giving may not have direct relationship with specific vocations, at least not to the extent that other gifts have. Giving has to do with sharing resources, not with earning them. The person who exercises the gift properly will do so with generosity and simplicity—he will not think lowly of those who receive his gifts, and he will give without regretting his decisions. Perhaps careers involving financial decision-making would be appropriate for such a person to consider.

Faith is present in the life of every Christian, but the gift of faith focuses beyond saving belief to a wonder-working faith. Of course, no one's faith *produces* a work of God (God Himself does that), but it sets the climate in which God is pleased to demonstrate His greatness.[7] Persons with this gift often are used to provide the challenge as a dynamic church attempts great things for God. They frequently do this by seeing beyond present difficulties to envision new accomplishments. Persons who find themselves contributing in this way to their church could have the gift of faith, and that gift may be accompanied by abilities that would have career applications. The ability to envision new products, new ways of doing things, new solutions for old problems, new organizations—the ability to see "what might be" can be an asset in vocational settings that require creativity.

Pastoring is a gift that is exercised within the church and probably has no corresponding functions outside the body of Christ. The term "pastor" refers not only to a gift, but to an office. Some may have the gift (nurturing, edifying in Christian life and growth) who do not have the office, but even these find expression for their gift within the church. One who thinks he has the gift and aspires to the office of pastor should look at the New Testament requirements and description of pastors. The office of pastor no doubt requires, in addition to the gift of pastoring, at least the gifts of teaching, exhortation, and administration. Probably gifts of evangelism and helps are indicated as necessary also.

Resembling the pastor's role, the gift of evangelism probably functions only within Christian service. One who has this gift will probably communicate the gospel in a simple, easily understood manner. Perhaps evangelists in the early church had itinerant ministries, introducing the gospel to an area, and then moving on to leave to the pastors the permanent task of building the

---

7. Gangel, p. 31.

believers into churches. Today, many Bible teachers and missionaries as well as evangelists demonstrate this gift.

Cautions

Spiritual gifts are God-given abilities for service within His church. Consequently, the presence of a spiritual gift does not automatically dictate a particular career outside Christian service. Some people have several spiritual gifts, and abilities other than spiritual gifts are required in most vocations. There does not seem to be a one-to-one relationship between spiritual gifts and specific careers.

Also, the spiritual gifts focus on people-related activities, and this focus should be expected since people and ideas (rather than things or data) comprise the thrust of the church's mission. Obviously, many careers exist that are not people (or idea) related, and knowledge of spiritual gifts would probably provide little or no help in choosing these vocations.

In spite of these cautions, however, our knowledge of our spiritual gifts *can help* us in career decisions because these gifts are part of our lives as Christians. Our decision-making model involves consideration of as much information about ourselves as possible, and certainly these gifts merit consideration along with other God-given abilities. While the gift or gifts we possess may not dictate a specific career, they must be considered if we are to understand ourselves as God-made people. And the greater our self-understanding, the better our career decisions will be.

As noted earlier, many Christians have given little thought to the topic of spiritual gifts and may have no idea what their particular gifts are. To them, this chapter may seem too idealistic to be of practical benefit. A responsibility rests upon each of us as Christians, however, to function within a church, whether or not we are making career choices. This church involvement necessitates the use of spiritual gifts. Knowing, developing, and using spiritual gifts should take priority over career decisions, for without participation in a local church, we cannot be all God intends us to be as Christians. (Suggestions for discovering our gifts were given earlier in this chapter.) Consequently, if we do not know or are not using our spiritual gifts, we need to correct these omissions before proceeding with career decision making.

7 *Circumstances*

"It's all a matter of luck—being at the right place at the right time." The student's remark expresses what is probably the most commonly held view of vocational choice. Many people who have had fulfilling careers will comment, "I guess I was just lucky." And people whose work experiences have been frustrating often complain, "I just didn't get any of the breaks." All of these statements are saying something about circumstances—they say that circumstances determine career direction.

Often Christians say essentially the same thing, only, of course, using a "sanctified vocabulary." These testify about finding "open doors" and "closed doors," and we hear how they discern God's will by finding just the right combination of "open doors." While it is difficult to know what is meant by an "open door" in every case, the phrase is usually used to describe favorable circumstances. Consequently, the "open door" guidance approach is one which allows circumstances to determine career decisions.

Obviously, numerous circumstances are involved in any decision, and career decisions are no exception. Yet, several questions remain. *How* shall circumstances be involved? Should they dictate, or should they only influence decision making? Should they be accepted, or overcome, or neither? Which circumstances are outside of ourselves, and which are under our control or influence? What is a circumstance? Answers to these questions are suggested in this chapter, and our approach will be to consider circumstances as *directing,* but not necessarily *dictating* career decisions.

What Are "Circumstances"?

When looking for God's will, we normally speak of *circumstances* as those events or conditions in our environment that have an impact on our decisions. It is commonly assumed that circumstances are environmental factors in the sense that they are outside of ourselves, factors over which we have no control.

Some research has shown that various social factors do exist which greatly influence career direction. The social status and wealth of the families into which we were born influence career choices, as do the abilities and limitations each of us has. These are not chance happenings, however. Their effects can be predicted fairly accurately and integrated into a responsible career decision.

Other circumstances in our social environment can have a more disruptive effect. The outbreak of war, for instance, will rearrange the career plans of hundreds of thousands of young men who may be drafted into military service. An economic recession usually forces many persons out of jobs, and inflation often prompts career homemakers to search for other jobs in order to increase the family income. The death of a spouse, either husband or wife, usually affects career decisions for the survivor. Automation can end some careers and expand others. Physical disabilities can occur quite outside our control, and these often require vocational adjustment.

Some circumstances, however, are really not outside ourselves or beyond our control. For instance, an aspiring physician might consider the failure to get into medical school an unfortunate "circumstance," and it might well be. However, it also could be the result of a failure to earn high enough college grades, or a failure to apply to enough medical schools, or some other personal factor. Or as another example, being released from a job due to automation may be a "circumstance" outside of one's control. But it could also be a result of a negligence in keeping up to date technically, a failure to foresee changes and retrain appropriately.

While some circumstances really do exist outside our control, and these really do influence career decisions, we should guard against assuming too quickly that we are at the mercy of these circumstances. These "circumstances" may well be self-induced conditions prompted by some oversight or negligence on our part. Further, the circumstance is usually far less important than our interpretation of and reaction to it.

Circumstances: Directing

Circumstances may direct career decisions because God is orderly. The One to whom we pray for guidance is not confused about His plan for His creation. He has overlooked no detail and has forgotten none of His children. His plan for our lives is perfectly coordinated with His will for His creation as a whole (Rom. 8:28). He is not only Lord of our individual lives, He is Lord of the universe.

Since the Lord of the universe is orderly, we might expect Him to arrange the circumstances surrounding our lives in a way that will encourage the accomplishment of His plan for us. As the psalmist reflected on the omniscience and omnipresence of God, he exclaimed,

Thou dost scrutinize my path and my lying down,
And art intimately acquainted with all my ways.
Thou hast enclosed me behind and before,
And laid Thy hand upon me (Ps. 139:3, 5).

This "enclosure" brings considerable security; it reminds us God is at work in the circumstances that affect our lives. We should not expect God to lead us, and then erect insurmountable barricades so we will be frustrated in our attempts to follow Him. We should anticipate His coordination of at least some circumstances with His plan for our lives.

In the light of the lordship of our God, it is quite inappropriate for us to talk about "luck," or "chance," or "fate," or "coincidences." All of these words denote an impersonal force that produces some unforeseen, unpredictable opportunity. This impersonal force concept is exactly opposite to the biblical belief of a God who is sovereignly active in His creation. Events may occur that the world might label as "lucky breaks," but we know them to be the handiwork of the orderly, personal God.

How then can these circumstances direct us?

First, circumstances can affect decisions by shaping the decider. Not only do the experiences of our lives develop us prior to facing career decisions, but also events during the decision time can influence our knowledge of ourselves. For instance, an illness during a crucial time may seem to direct us in a decision, but its guidance may come from the fact that it forces an examination and reordering of personal priorities. The circumstance in this case affects the priorities of the decider, which, in turn affects the decision.

Second, circumstances may correct us when we are earnestly seeking for and trying to accomplish God's will, but make a mistake. Perhaps circumstances will function to point out new alternatives, previously undiscovered options that include God's plan. Since God looks on our hearts and not merely on our outward actions, we expect Him to deal with His mistaken children differently than He does His rebellious ones. Christians who are stubbornly refusing to do His will should expect chastisement, but those who genuinely desire God's direction and make some mistake in understanding it ought to expect gentle correction. Often, God can use circumstances to nudge us out of mistaken ideas and into His perfect plan. For example, David Livingstone responded to God's leading toward a missionary ministry, but he thought he was to go to China. God redirected him by using a circumstance—a war between Britain and China—so that he turned to Africa. God used the circumstance to force an examination of new options, but not to punish a rebellious servant.

One of the most frequent uses of circumstances is the practice of "putting out a fleece." Referring to Gideon's experiment of asking for a wet fleece on dry ground and vice versa, this practice seeks a circumstance as a sign to confirm God's leading. A closer examination of Gideon's actions (Judges 6) shows that he was not setting an example for us to follow. We are nowhere commanded to follow his example with the fleeces, and we generally get into trouble when we make the exceptional experience of someone a rule of faith for everyone. Gideon put out his fleece because he did not trust either God's Word to him or the sign God had already given him. Gideon's faith and greatness are shown in many ways in Scripture, but his experience with the fleeces is not one of them.

Usually, asking God for some confirming sign is an indication that we are failing to follow faithfully a reasonable decision making process. It is much easier, of course, to follow some spectacular sign than it is to research alternatives, examine ourselves, study Scripture, and make a decision based on biblical criteria. So "putting out a fleece" can be a sign of mental or spiritual laziness. God may sometimes give confirming signs, as He did with Gideon, but we have no assurance that He will. And if He does, we should be aware that He is not rewarding our strong faith but patiently tolerating our weakness.

Like Gideon, when we ask God for a confirming circumstance, our fleece is usually unrelated to our decision. One person testified he asked God to make it rain on the following Tuesday if he was to purchase a new car. This was to be his sign of God's approval of his decision. Of course, he had not carefully evaluated his transportation needs and financial condition in the light of biblical principles of stewardship. Had he done so, he would have had no need to ask for rain. A student reported that he had asked for a grant of $1000 as a sign of whether to continue in college. When his grant finally came, it amounted to $750, and so the student felt he had to leave college. In fact, however, he had not examined numerous other alternatives, including the likelihood that the Lord's will was for him to work part time to earn the additional money.

Relying on circumstances as signs, then, shows both distrust and laziness. Eyrich and Strickland have commented, "To ask for a sign, even in terms of having a good or peaceful feeling, is requiring God to second His own motion, a testing of God to see if what He has said is actually true in practice."[1]

---

1. Howard Eyrich and Bruce Strickland. "Counseling the Decision Makers," *Journal of Pastoral Practice* 1 (Winter, 1977): 36.

Using circumstances to prompt self-examination or to suggest additional alternatives can be appropriate. The events surrounding our lives and decisions are within the control of the Lord who is leading us. Consequently, these circumstances can help us find the proper direction for our decisions.

Circumstances: Not Dictating

While circumtances can give us direction, serious problems arise when we allow circumstances to *dictate* our decisions. This dictatorship occurs when we think that some circumstance *demands* a particular decision, and we fail to search for alternatives.

Unfortunately, many Christians only look at "circumstantial evidence" when making career decisions and totally neglect the self-appraisal process explained earlier. Learning that the job market for teachers is tight, for instance, is enough to cause many students to decide to leave teacher-education programs in college. The job market, of course, must be considered, but rarely is it a circumstance that would *dictate* such a decision. A tight job market does *not* mean that no jobs will be available; it means that the competition will be more rigorous because there are more job seekers than job openings. Tens of thousands of openings annually could exist within this tight job market. If the decision-making process indicates teaching, then the job market situation should not change that decision. Rather, it should challenge the prospective teacher to make the best record possible while in college to insure that he will be among the best qualified candidates for the openings. The circumstance is considered, but it does not dictate—it does not replace the decision-making process which focuses on what God has done in the life of the prospective teacher to prepare him for teaching.

Following are several reasons why circumstances should not *dictate* decisions for Christians.

First, circumstances are subject to interpretation. They do not speak for themselves. The circumstances surrounding Jonah's flight from God's will could be interpreted to indicate he was doing the right thing. He found a ship going just where he wanted to go, leaving when he wanted to leave, with room for him aboard, and with the right ticket price (Jonah 1). The circumstances seemed favorable, but the decision was wrong. The meaning we attach to the circumstance becomes far more important than the circumstance itself. College students who run out of money can illustrate this principle. A student may not have the money necessary for the next semester's costs, and so he interprets this circumstance as dictating his withdrawal from college. Yet, it is amazing how many students withdraw for financial reasons who have never even inquired from their college's financial aid office regarding financial assistance. They interpret their "circumstance" to mean withdrawal, while the same circumstance could also be interpreted as an indication to apply for another grant, an educational loan, a work-study job, a deferred-payment plan, or some other alternative. Circumstances by themselves cannot dictate because they have meaning only when interpreted.

Second, the principle of selective perception operates in interpreting circumstances, and this principle limits the dictating potential of the circumstances. Our perception is the process of becoming aware of our circumstances through receiving and organizing the evidence received by our senses. Some evidence we may choose to ignore, and some evidence we may organize differently than others would. Some people see obstacles wherever they look and become discouraged. Others in similar circumstances see opportunities and become challenged. Our background and experiences develop a mind-set which filters the information our senses receive and organizes this for attaching meaning. Circumstances, therefore, cannot dictate decisions because they do not dictate how they will be perceived.

Third, circumstances may be used to test our commitment to following God. The apostle Paul encountered many types of opposition when seeking to fulfill his calling, and the result was a strenghthening and refining of his own life (II Cor. 11:23-33; 12:10). We often make the mistake of thinking that favorable circumstances indicate an "open door," and that formidable obstacles indicate a "closed door." In fact, however, adverse circumstances may be placed in our path, not to change our direction, but to test and thereby strengthen our commitment. When Paul wrote to the Corinthian church about his work at Ephesus, he said, "For a great door and effectual is opened unto me, and there are many adversaries" (I Cor. 16:9). The presence of "many adversaries," or unfavorable circumstances, was not enough to convince Paul that the door was closed. Rather, he defined the open door as one in which much would be accomplished ("effectual") in the presence of many obstacles.

Similarly, most of us probably know or have read of persons who have achieved much in life by overcoming seemingly insurmountable problems. The crippled youngster who becomes an Olympic champion perhaps epitomizes this achievement, and multitudes have accomplished much in similar but less spectacular ways. The polio victim who becomes the scientist, the blind attorney, the quadraplegic counselor, the handicapped physician— they all tell us that adverse circumstances do not dictate career decisions. But we should not look only at physical circumstances. Many have overcome tremendous emotional distress, social or economic disadvantages, or family discouragements to live fulfilled and successful lives. If circumstances were always allowed to dictate career decisions, such success stories would not exist.

A fourth problem with allowing circumstances to dictate decisions is that it is inconsistent with the life of faith. Habakkuk's message "The just shall live by his faith" is quoted in the New Testament and applied to our salvation, showing that we live by faith and not by works. But in Habakkuk's day, the application might have been slightly different. The believing remnant in Judah were discouraged because they saw violence, injustice, and gross depravity on every hand. Habakkuk prophesied that God would bring the more wicked Chaldeans against Judah in punishment of Judah's iniquity. Certainly the circumstances offered no hope for living or encouragement for righteousness. But the just were not to live by their perception of their circumstances; the just were to live by faith. They were to believe God, and act accordingly, in spite of their circumstances.

When we live by faith, we do not merely react to circumstances. We are to see beyond hindrances or distractions because our commitment is to God, not to the circumstances of this life. A life-style which only reacts to circumstances requires no faith, commitment, or obedience. Commitment to Jesus Christ often requires us to *act* in the midst of circumstances, not merely to *react* to them.

Living by faith involves living by our understanding of God and His Word. Consequently, we are not to see our circumstances as fatalistic forces that cannot be successfully overcome, if need be. Circumstances are often temporary conditions that will wield little impact in the future. But living by faith focuses on God and His purposes, which transcend time.

Summary

How then can we use circumstances in making God-honoring career decisions? Circumstances can direct and influence us, because the same God who is leading us is also the Lord over the circumstances and the events of our lives. But circumstances cannot automatically dictate our decisions because our interpretation of the circumstances is fallible and because the circumstances may be intended to test us rather than guide us.

Rather than drifting through life by reacting to circumstances, the Christian can make career plans by prayerfully considering what the orderly, personal God has already done in his life. Our interests, abilities, limitations, experiences, values, etc., provide a much better basis for career decisions than do our perceptions of our ever-changing circumstances.

8 The Call

Does God call us to specific careers?

Most secular textbooks on career development that include a discussion of various career theories mention a "divine selection theory." Usually labeled "antiquated" and assigned to a Middle Ages mentality, this theory proposes that each person is both chosen for a career and informed of his fate by a Supreme Being. Naturally, this approach is ridiculed widely today because it is seen as too deterministic and it supposedly robs us of autonomy in career choice.

Ironically, each career theory proposed in place of divine selection represents a more severe form of determinism. Theories of career choice have been focused at heredity, socio-economic factors, psychological limits, and the developmental process, and all of these propose one type of determinism or another. The ridicule focused on divine selection, then, comes not from its determinism, per se. Rather, it arises from the assumption that God does not exist, or at least is not personally active, and that man is the sole determiner and measure of all things.

We should not be surprised when a culture that has tried to excise all consideration of God from its thinking rebels against the idea that God would be involved in career choice. As Christians, we may not agree completely with the divine selection theory as stated above, but we do believe in the existence of an orderly, personal God.

Since God is orderly, we can safely conclude that His plan includes His children, those who have been saved by His grace through faith in Jesus Christ. It is inconceivable that God would have an orderly plan and fail to include in it the work of His creatures, especially those whom He has redeemed. That God has a plan for our lives follows naturally from the fact that He is orderly.

Also, since God is personal, we can safely conclude that He has a personal interest and concern for each of us. He has personally been involved in our lives—forming us, developing us, saving us, leading us, gifting us. It is unthinkable that He would not guide us in such a crucial matter as career choice, but rather leave that to some impersonal, fatalistic force. And it is also unthinkable that a personal God would have a plan for our lives and wish to conceal it from us.

How, then, does God inform us of His will for us? The term "call" has been used to denote the process in which He enlightens us regarding His plan for our careers. And sometimes a "call" is limited only to professional ministry careers (e.g., pastor, missionary, etc.), giving the impression that those in other careers have had no calling.

We are then faced with at least two pressing questions: "What is a 'call'?" and "How do I know if I have been called?" The discussion in the remainder of this chapter may not answer these questions directly, but it will provide at least a framework for considering them.

Call to Salvation

The vast majority of Scripture passages that speak of God's "call" refer to His call to salvation and to holy living. Concerning our salvation, for example, the Bible states that we are *called* out of darkness into His light (I Pet. 2:9), *called* to repentance (Acts 2:38-39), *called* by the gospel (II Thess. 2:14), *called* into fellowship with Jesus Christ (I Cor. 1:9), *called* into the body of Christ (Col. 3:15), *called* into His kingdom (I Thess. 2:12), and *called* to eternal life (I Tim. 6:12; Heb. 9:15).

As Christians, we are *called* to be saints (I Cor. 1:2), denoting not only our salvation but also holy living following our conversion. A call to holiness should be expected when we consider the fact that it is the Holy One who calls us (I Pet. 1:15).

Every Christian, then, has received God's call. Without it, we would never be saved (Rom. 8:30). But this *call* concerns salvation, not career choice. Perhaps this biblical emphasis on the call to salvation should remind us that God's will for our lives focuses much more on the people we *are*, rather than on how we earn a living.

Call to Christian Service Careers

The question "Are you called?" is normally asked of persons planning to enter Christian service careers, especially within evangelical circles. Most must assert and somehow prove this calling before being ordained or commissioned for missionary service.

The expression "full-time Christian service" is not used in this chapter because every Christian is called to serve Christ all the time regardless of his career. In place of this inadequate expression, we will refer to "Christian service careers" and "professional ministry careers." Both of these terms more adequately convey the concept of serving Christ in a vocational manner. While every Christian is to serve Christ and minister to fellow believers, some are called to do so in a career sense, and they earn their living by their ministries. These we are calling "Christian service careers." "Secular careers" are those in which one's living is earned by functions other than ministry. While it is probably impossible to draw a clear line between the two, the Scripture does indicate that there is some difference, and that this difference involves the matter of earning the living (I Cor. 9:14). "Secular careers" are neither less spiritual nor less sacred than Christian service careers (as shown in chapter 2), for the spirituality of one's work is determined not by the content of the work, but rather by the spirituality of the worker.

Although the biblical passages are relatively scarce, there is sufficient revelation to warrant the assertion that a call should precede entry to a Christian service career. The Old Testament priests and prophets occupied their positions by God's choice, not by their own selection. He was speaking of priests when the writer of Hebrews stated, "No one takes the honor to himself, but receives it when he is called by God, even as Aaron was" (5:4). Amos recounts his own call to the prophetic ministry in this way: "I am a herdsman and a grower of sycamore figs. But the Lord took me from following the flock and said to me, 'Go prophecy to My people Israel' " (7:14-15). Those who represented God did so at His initiative and direction, not their own.

In the New Testament, Jesus chose the disciples who would become the apostles (Luke 6:13 ff.). While each one had an eagerness to follow Him, no one became a disciple/apostle by volunteering. Rather, they were specifically called by Jesus Christ to their ministries. Similarly, Paul speaks of being *called* to be an apostle (Rom. 1:1; I Cor. 1:1), and within that office, *called* to preach (Acts 16:10). He was "appointed a preacher and an apostle and a teacher" (II Tim. 1:11). Consequently, he felt constrained by God to such an extent that he exclaimed, "Woe is me if I do not preach the gospel" (I Cor. 9:16). Paul's calling came, of course, through the extraordinary means of a vision (Acts 9), a means God used only occasionally in Bible times and not at all today.

Most of the biblical data concerning the call to ministry pertains to offices no longer functioning (priest, prophet, apostle). Consequently, the concepts we have of current calls to ministry are usually the applications we make from the formerly functioning offices to the presently functioning ones. We may infer that God selects evangelists and pastor/teachers today as He did the prophets and apostles, since He lists them together as His gifts to the church (Eph. 4:11). He does "send" persons to preach (Rom. 10:15), and

91

He plans for those who preach the gospel to make their living by their ministry (I Cor. 9:14).

Some argument for a call might rightly be made from the nature of Christian service careers. To represent the Lord without His call to do so would be presumptuous. Wagner says,

> It is incongruous to think that an ambassador would go to a country as a representative of his homeland without being sent. To take such a position would be unthinkable. This is even more true in the ministry. . . . To go, without being sent, is to walk in failure.[1]

But the Scripture simply does not present as much emphasis on the calling of pastor/teachers as it does on the calling of persons to the offices of priest, prophet, and apostle (and it makes no mention whatever of calls to non-preaching ministries such as medical missions, Christian school teaching, writing, etc.).

Does this mean that pastor/teachers and evangelists need not be "called" of God? Does it mean that medical missionaries, Christian educators, etc., are not called? The biblical evidence, though not abundant, gives sufficient basis for believing that God *does call* persons into His service. We are mistaken if we try to justify present day "calls" by equating present ministries with the apostolic and prophetic offices (e.g., missionary = apostle; pastor = prophet), since these offices were to serve the church only in its infancy (Eph. 2:20). A preferable approach would be to define this calling as *God's personal guidance through which He enlightens us regarding His plan for our lives*. While none of His guidance will ever contradict His Word, it is probably unnecessary to pin every aspect of His plan for every one of His children to a specific Bible verse. And so we will focus on this guidance rather than trying to find specific verses to justify calls to every type of ministry.

How, then, can we know if we are called into some Christian service career? We must admit that the New Testament does not describe the mechanics of a call, nor does it give a concise checklist for recognizing calls. The following suggestions, then, are based in part on human experience in addition to divine revelation, but perhaps they still have some value in that God may choose to grant similar experiences in calling people to similar tasks.

The first indication usually is a consciousness within our own minds that God desires this for us. Lloyd-Jones has stated,

---

1. Charles U. Wagner, *The Pastor, His Life and Work* (Schaumberg, Ill.: Regular Baptist Press, 1976). p. 1.

A call generally starts in the form of a consciousness within one's own spirit, some disturbance in the realm of the spirit, that your mind is being directed . . . it is God dealing with you, and God acting upon you by His Spirit; it is something you become aware of rather than something you do.[2]

This awareness is more a mental conviction than an emotional upheaval. The work of God within the mind produces both a desire and a sense of necessity. We should expect Him to give us a desire for ministry if that is His plan. Paul wrote, "If a man *desire* the office of a bishop, he desireth a good work" (I Tim. 3:1). As this desire matures, it strengthens into the kind of constraint Paul felt in his ministry when he said, "for I am under compulsion; for woe is me if I do not preach the gospel" (I Cor. 9:16). The guidance of God is recognized as a "divine initiative, a solemn communication of the divine will . . .which leaves a man no alternative."[3]

Another indication of God's leadership into a Christian service career is the insight and testimony of godly persons. For instance, the church members at Antioch recognized God's call of Barnabas and Saul to missionary service at least as quickly as the missionaries themselves did. This confirmation apparently was based not on some mysterious hunches, but on an evaluation of service already performed for the cause of Christ (Acts 13:1-3). If an inclination toward ministry is not verified by at least some godly acquaintances, a "call" should be doubted.

Since ministry serves to bring people into a relationship with God, we might expect called persons to have a right relationship themselves with God and with others. It is doubtful that God would press into His service one who despised Him or His Word. A desire to know God and to handle His Word competently should be expected in the life of one called (as in every Christian's life). Those in the early church who were in career ministries purposed to devote themselves "to prayer, and to the ministry of the Word" (Acts 6:4). A call to ministry is a call to study.

Similarly, a right relationship with others is essential, and many of the personal qualifications listed for pastors are aimed at good interpersonal relations (I Tim. 3; Titus 1). While not expecting everyone's love, understanding, or approval, one called into a ministry career will have a genuine concern for others. Lloyd-Jones writes,

The true call always includes a concern about others, an interest in

---

2. D. Martyn Lloyd-Jones, *Preaching and Preachers* (Grand Rapids: Zondervan Publishing House, 1971), p. 104.

3. J. H. Jowett, *The Preacher, His Life and Work* (New York: Harper & Brothers, 1912), p. 19.

them, a realization of their lost estate and condition, and a desire to do something about them, and to tell them the message and point them to the way of salvation. This is an essential part of the call; and it is important, particularly as a means whereby we may check ourselves.[4]

A call to the pastorate in particular must involve a serious examination of and commitment to the qualifications for pastors outlined in I Timothy 3 and Titus 1. Failure to meet these qualifications exempts one from pastoral office, no matter how strongly he may feel called! It may be noteworthy that "feeling called" is *not* listed among pastoral qualifications in either I Timothy or Titus. This omission does not mean a call is unnecessary. Rather, it probably indicates that these qualifications are criteria for determining whether one is called. While there is no concise checklist for determining a call, these qualifications probably are as close to being such a list as anything we have. Interestingly, these criteria focus on personal traits and interpersonal relationships more than on specific aptitudes. The only vocational aptitude listed is the ability to teach. Spiritual maturity is emphasized, along with personal traits that demonstrate this maturity. Right relationships within both family and community are likewise emphasized. Consideration of these lists of qualifications will likely produce a sense of unworthiness or insufficiency, but we should be reminded that God promises growth and development when we follow Him faithfully.

Spiritual gifts can serve as reliable indicators of a call to professional ministry since they are God-given abilities for service. The presence or absence of these gifts can therefore indicate appropriate roles within the church. Pastors, in particular, should have the gift of pastoring, which involves a spiritual protection and nurture of other believers. Additionally, the qualifications and office description given to the pastorate in the New Testament would require at least the gifts of teaching, exhortation, and administration, and probably evangelism and helps also (see chapter 6). Similarly, other Christian service careers require specific spiritual gifts, and if these are not present, at least in undeveloped form, a call should be doubted.

If God seems to direct us into a career of ministry, then, we should examine not only the inward, subjective leading, but also the outward, objective facts. Some of the following questions may prove helpful in determining God's call:

Subjective criteria:

Do I think I am called?

---

4. Lloyd-Jones, pp. 104-5.

Do I desire this ministry?
Do I feel I *must* be involved in this ministry?

Objective criteria:

Do I meet the appropriate qualifications?
Do I have confirmation from other believers?
Do I have the necessary spiritual gifts?
Do I have a genuine concern for other people?

Such an examination can assure us that we are placing appropriate emphasis on both subjective and objective aspects of our decision.

And since both subjective and objective aspects are involved, a call from God does not mean that the investigative and decision making processes outlined earlier are unnecessary. A call does not decrease the necessity of knowing about ourselves; if anything, it increases the urgency of self-understanding. Neither does a call render unnecessary an understanding of what is involved in different ministry careers. Certainly, a proper decision making process is imperative in order to determine if one is truly called, and also to ascertain the nature and direction of the call. To say, therefore, "I can't be bothered with making career decisions because I have been called" is to take a short-sighted approach which shows a lack of understanding both of a "calling" and of career decision making. The career decision process outlined earlier is appropriate for those who "feel called." It will assist in determining, clarifying, and responding to the call.

We have already seen that the call to a Christian service career is neither mysterious nor irrational. The Scripture records visions and other miraculous events connected with calling persons to offices that operated prior to the completion of Scripture (priests, prophets, apostles, and Old Testament leaders like Moses). *Nowhere* are we told that His calling of persons to continuing offices (e.g., pastor/teacher, missionary/evangelist, deacon) was accompanied by such supernatural signs and wonders, even in New Testament times! And *nowhere* are we told to expect such signs. What we should expect, however, are (1) God's equipping by granting grace for meeting biblical qualifications, (2) the Spirit's gifting for accomplishing the calling, and (3) God's implanting of a desire for ministry. In fact, many testify that their calling was not a sudden, spectacular event, but rather, a gradually deepening conviction and a process in which God's work in their life was progressively clarified.

Calls to Other Careers

While the Scriptures give evidence that God calls persons into Christian service careers, it does not use the same terminology regarding other careers. Paul was called to be an apostle, for instance, but although he was also a tentmaker, he does not say he was "called" to tentmaking. Similarly, God's selection of priests and prophets receives emphasis, while we don't customarily read of Him "calling" people to farming or to business. This difference has led to two common mistakes: (1) mystifying the call to Christian service so that it is encased with awe and exempted from rational decision making; (2) assigning all other careers to a non-call, non-spiritual status.

We have used the word "call" to describe the process whereby God enlightens us regarding His plan for our careers. When understood in this sense, we see that God's guidance into other careers is just as much a "calling" as is His leading into professional ministry. While the outcomes may be quite different, the process is probably similar in both cases. Both require considerable prayer and trust in God for His guidance. Both should involve a rigorous self-examination as well as a thorough study of alternatives, evaluated by a Scripturally-based value system. Both should seek to utilize the appropriate gifts and talents placed in the life by God. Both should include the strong, inward conviction that one is in the plan of God, doing God's will from the heart.

While many Christian accountants, homemakers, coal miners, policemen, etc., may not refer to their careers as "callings," if they are pursuing their careers with assurance they are in God's plan, they have as much right to consider their careers "callings" as anyone else. In fact, the word "vocation" is taken from the Latin *vocatio,* meaning "calling." Whoever speaks of his "vocation," therefore, is acknowledging his "calling." The Christian who is faithfully walking with his Lord acknowledges that his vocation (calling) has come from God, not from himself, or from his world, or from blind fate.

While the Christian fireman or nurse or scientist may not be able to justify his profession by pointing to a specific verse in the Bible, he can be assured that he is in God's plan as a result of God's personal leading. Following the career decision plan in chapters 3-7 will normally assure that we take into account all that God has placed in our lives to indicate His plan for our vocations. If we mistakenly think of His leading or call as a sudden, spectacular event, few of us will ever consider ourselves called to secular careers. But God's leading is normally neither sudden nor spectacular. His leading usually occurs on a day-by-day basis, teaching us about His work in our lives and guiding us through our experiences. Receiving God's guidance, like all of the Christian life, is not as much sudden spurts as it is consistent, faithful living.

Higher Callings, Lower Callings

Sermons meant to challenge people to enter Christian service careers frequently refer to these careers as "God's highest calling." While usually not stated, the clear implication is that other careers are lower, and therefore, somewhat inferior callings.

The Scripture does present Christian service as a high calling. The pastoral office, for instance, is described as a "fine work" (I Tim. 3:1), and being placed in the ministry requires evidence of faithfulness (I Tim. 1:12). There should be no question that ministering the Word of God to people constitutes a high calling, and that offices within the church involve considerable responsibility and authority.

As high a calling as the ministry is, however, we simply cannot support from Scripture a higher calling/lower calling division. Rather, we see just the opposite in Scripture. When we study the biblical value of work (chapter 2), we see that God values all types of careers. A recognition that God is sovereign in dispensing gifts, abilities, limitations, interests, etc., reminds us that He guides His people into many different careers. Following His leadership and fulfilling His plan is a genuinely spiritual endeavor, regardless of the vocation involved. Ultimately, a higher and lower calling division reflects on the person of God, for after all, He is the One doing the calling.

Unfortunately, the appeals to "God's highest calling," though well intentioned, can have sinful effects. These appeals can engender pride, as an artificial hierarchy is erected among Christians, some of whom are "higher" than others. Even the fact that church offices can involve authority does not create the hierarchy which places some people "higher" or "better" than others. Also, appeals to "God's highest calling" can coerce sensitive believers into Christian service careers apart from God's leadership, simply because they mistakenly think they cannot experience God's best or His blessing otherwise. Further, these appeals frequently intimidate faithful Christians who have conscientiously followed God's leadership into secular careers.

Rather than thinking of higher and lower callings, we should recognize that any calling from God is a high calling, simply because He made it. The determining factor is not the content of the call, but rather, the One who made it and the faithfulness of the one receiving it. If there is such a thing as a "lower calling," it is a career chosen out of a wrong attitude or a rebellion against God's leading. And once again, the determining factor is not the career itself, but the wrong attitude and unfaithfulness of the person.

Summary

When we believe in a personal, orderly God, we assume that He will work directly with us in granting guidance. God specifically chooses, prepares, and calls those whom He wishes to be in Christian service careers. And since this choice, preparation, and guidance is a reflection of His nature, He works in much the same manner in leading Christians into secular careers. The involvement of the eternal God, the Lord of heaven and earth, in guiding us in career choices constitutes those careers as high callings, regardless of the careers themselves.

9 *Being a Whole Person*

Her words would have been startling enough had she been the only one to use them. The bright college woman, faced with a serious yet typical dilemma, spoke what has become a common cry when she said, "I have to decide—I can either get married, or I can make something out of my life." Her dilemma, however, was self-imposed and unnecessary because it came from two glaring errors in her thinking. First, she was mistakenly compartmentalizing her life and therefore missing a sense of wholeness. Second, she was ascribing too much importance to her career plans, expecting her career to fill too many needs for her.

God's concern for us encompasses all that we are, and His will involves us as a whole people, not merely as vocational units. As we have seen earlier (chapter 3), God's leadership involves whole persons. Yet, many continually divide their lives into separate compartments—considering job, marriage, child-rearing, spiritual life, recreation, etc., as completely separate. This unnatural division almost always results eventually in frustration, particularly when the "compartments" are as far apart as the girl above saw in her life. It had not occurred to her that marriage and "making something out of her life" were not mutually exclusive, but could be either identical or complementary goals. Career homemakers, for instance, "make something of themselves" in and through marriage itself. Others express themselves in careers and in marriage without building barriers between career and marriage.

A common instance of this compartmentalization is the artificial distinction between sacred and secular aspects of life. Those making such a division consider some of their activities for Christ, and some for themselves. Such divisions, however, are most inconsistent with biblical Christianity. Since we are to do everything we do to the glory of God, there is no such thing as a "secular activity" for the Christian. Arthur Holmes has well stated,

> Evidently work—even the "secular"—is a divine calling, so that religious devotion is not confined to the inner life or to those times we directly address ourselves to God. There should be no dichotomy of

99

secular and sacred. Everything a man does becomes sacred when he does it for the glory of God.[1]

God is not interested in using or leading fragments of our lives; His will concerns us as whole persons. Dividing our lives into separate segments leads to a fractured existence, not to healthy living. God's sanctifying grace is intended for all of life, as Paul understood when he prayed, "And the very God of peace sanctify you *wholly* [entirely]; and I pray God your *whole* spirit and soul and body be preserved blameless unto the coming of our Lord Jesus Christ" (I Thess. 5:23). Paul could think of no aspect of human life which should be deprived of God's enriching grace. We should be cautious, therefore, about subdividing our lives and assuming we will gain fulfillment (or lose it) in each compartment separately.

A second common mistake is that of ascribing too much importance to our careers, elevating them to cultic status and worshiping at the shrine of careerism. While our careers are vitally important in that they are inextricably connected to our sense of identity (chapter 2), they do not totally comprise identity. The girl who could "make something of herself" only by means of a career was no doubt compartmentalizing her life and placing an undue emphasis on the career compartment to the neglect of the others. Commitment to a career as the only means of personal fulfillment will lead to frustration because God has made us to function as *whole* persons. Devotion to careerism can also produce an obsession with advancement to the point that other important values are sacrificed to "get ahead."

It may seem strange that after emphasizing the importance of our careers in all the previous chapters, the focus now appears to shift toward limiting this importance. Actually, what is necessary is a proper balance that accounts for both the importance and the limitations of our careers. The importance is undeniable since it is evident from Scripture. And Scripture also shows us that life is more than work.

With this balance in mind, going through a career decision process can produce genuine growth for all of life. The more we know about ourselves, the more we can find genuine fulfillment in all of our activities. And more importantly, the greater our self-knowledge, the greater is our potential for glorifying God with all our "spirit and soul and body." The proper use of the self-knowledge required for the decision making process will not merely make us better workers. It will make us better people.

Maintaining this balance also keeps us conscious of the fact that every facet of our lives interacts with the other facets. We, then, do not focus on

---

1. Arthur Holmes, *All Truth Is God's Truth* (Grand Rapids: Wm. B. Eerdmans Publishing Co., 1977), p. 26.

activity in one "compartment" as if it is entirely separate from others. Spiritual condition, for instance, surely affects job performance, and career satisfaction usually influences family relationships. Realizing these relationships leads to the understanding that God's plan encompasses all we are and consequently all we do. He does not intend to lead us in career choices without any plan for the remainder of our lives.

Throughout this book, the emphasis on thinking has been repeated. Career choice for Christians is a cognitive process. It is not primarily mystical or emotional, although mysticism and emotion are frequently confused with spirituality. Genuine spirituality, however, involves God-controlled thinking. Consequently, we read, "Commit thy works unto the Lord, and thy thoughts [plans] shall be established" (Prov. 16:3). Eyrich and Strickland have observed the following:

> The point at which God directs our decision-making is in the rational process, i.e., as the God-given ability to reason is used. . . . Here faith enters the picture. As the Christian commits his works to God and inputs all possible data (including his emotional reactions and willful desires), he is responsible to believe that God will establish (direct) his thoughts so that when he must make the decision he can rest assured that God has guided him.[2]

As we seek to integrate our life's various facets so that we really are whole persons, our thinking becomes the means of integration. What we know and how we think determines not only our career choices, but also the direction of our lives as whole people. And our thoughts are guided by God to the extent that we consciously obey Him in our works (Prov. 16:3).

But the Christian need not be content with knowing what God expects, or with knowing only facts. As Christians our knowledge goes infinitely further; we know God Himself. And isn't this knowledge of God crucial in knowing His will? How do we know the will of anyone, really, except by knowing him as a person. Consequently, Margaret Erb has summarized this knowledge as follows:

> As I have studied the Scriptures, I have been convinced that the men of God knew His will so thoroughly simply because they knew God so well.[3]

And so, throughout our thinking, our research, our analysis, our evaluating, our deciding—throughout all this, we need to be growing in our relationship

---

2. Howard Eyrich and Bruce Strickland, "Counseling the Decision Makers," *Journal of Pastoral Practice* 1 (Winter, 1977): 37.

3. Margaret Erb, "God Has a Plan," in *Essays on Guidance* (Downers Grove, Ill.: InterVarsity Press, 1968), p. 7.

with the Lord Himself. Knowing God does not mean we are relieved from the thinking tasks outlined in the previous chapters. But knowing God does mean our thinking will be affected to conform to His will. He Himself will shape our thinking. When we commit ourselves to knowing God's will we thereby commit ourselves to knowing God well.

ACTIVITIES FOR PERSONAL INVENTORY

1. From previous exercises (chapters 4 and 5), select and list below your strongest interests, abilities, and values. Then list as many careers as you can think of that would combine your strongest interests, abilities, and values.

Interests	*Abilities*	*Values*
_____	_____	_____
_____	_____	_____
_____	_____	_____
_____	_____	_____
_____	_____	_____
_____	_____	_____
_____	_____	_____

Career Alternatives

_____

_____

_____

_____

_____

_____

_____

2. Assume that you can design a job to fit you exactly—your interests, abilities, limitations, values, etc. In the space below, write a short classified ad for this job such as you might find in the "help wanted" section of a newspaper.

Help Wanted: _____

_____

_____

_____

_____

_____

_____

3. Where are you now in your own decision process? List below the specific information you need to advance to the next stage of the decision making model.

Present status: _____

Information needed: _____

_____

_____

_____

_____

_____

_____

4. List below the personal/spiritual traits you hope to have 10 years from now. How will your present career choice help you develop or strengthen these traits?

Trait	*Career Influence*
_____	_____
_____	_____
_____	_____
_____	_____
_____	_____
_____	_____

5. Complete the following sentence to the best of your ability using your present knowledge and values.

When my life ends, I will consider my life to have been successful if

RESOURCES FOR ADDITIONAL DEVELOPMENT

Career Information

1. *Occupational Outlook Handbook* ($8.00)

   Order from: Superintendent of Documents
   U.S. Government Printing Office
   Washington, D.C. 20402

   Most libraries and school guidance offices have copies.

2. Professional associations publish literature on the careers they represent. Addresses of these associations are listed in *The Encyclopedia of Associations* (Gale Research Co.), available in most libraries.

3. Your state's employment service may publish career descriptions.

4. Your local Civil Service commission office can give you information on government careers, including the publication *Federal Career Directory*.

5. The New York Life Insurance Company (51 Madison Avenue, New York, New York 10010) has published and distributes without charge a series of informative career brochures.

6. *Your Job: Survival or Satisfaction* by Jerry and Mary White (Zondervan Publishing House, 1977) gives a good description of several careers (including homemaking) and is written from a Christian perspective.

7. For information on Christian service careers, contact your local church, your denomination's headquarters, or specific mission agencies in which you are interested.

Career Textbooks and Workbooks

1. *Christian Career Planning,* by John Bradley (Multnomah Press, 1977). This is a text and workbook written from a Christian perspective. It also includes helpful information on job searches and resumes.

2. *PATH: A Career Workbook for Liberal Arts Students,* by Howard Figler (Carroll Press, 1975). Probably the most comprehensive workbook available, *PATH* is helpful particularly for persons with broad or diverse interests. Although not a Christian approach, it uses the values of the reader in its decision model.

Job Search Information

1. *Christian Career Planning,* by John Bradley (Multnomah Press, 1977) includes helpful information on interviews and resumes.

105

2. *Career Development for the College Student,* edited by Philip Dunphy (Carroll Press, 1973) includes information on resumes, letters, interviews, and adjustment to a new job.

3. *The Resume Workbook,* by Carolyn Nutter (Carroll Press, 1970), is a complete guide to resume writing and includes numerous samples.

4. *College Placement Annual,* published annually by the College Placement Council (P.O. Box 2263, Bethlehem, Penna. 18001). Available at most colleges and military bases, it gives helpful job search strategies and lists approximately 1300 companies and government agencies and their current personnel needs.

5. *What Color Is Your Parachute?* by Richard N. Bolles (Ten Speed Press, 1978), is not written from a Christian perspective, but gives excellent suggestions for creative job hunting methods.